PAT AND BOB
TRIP
THE LIGHT FANTASTIC

DR. ROBERT F. BRODSKY
PATRICIA W. BRODSKY

Being Annnals of Travel in
North And South America
Europe
North Africa
The Middle East
Russia And Asia

PAT AND BOB *TRIP* THE LIGHT FANTASTIC

For information contact Foxbro Press at 650 W. Harrison Ave.
Claremont, CA 91711, rfoxbro@aol.com, or (909) 626 2050

ISBN - 10: 1492747769
ISBN - 13: 9781492747765

Library of Congress Control Number: 2014913983

Printed in the United States of America
CreateSpace Independent Publishing Platform
North Charleston, South Carolina

DEDICATION

This book is dedicated to our favorite travelling companions who joined us on our many forays into foreign lands by land or by river boat or by ocean liner. We took several trips to South America, Mexico, Egypt, and Israel with Don and Donna Newbrough of Ames, Iowa. Likewise, we sight-saw in Israel, the US West Coast, and Hawaii with cousins Susan – nee Stern (and Dick) Rosenberg of Haifa; many cruises and land visits with Connie Voss and Janet Hicklin of Houston; with Kim Williams of Ames and Pat's aunt, Marge (and Frank) Clabaugh to Alaska/Canada; with Howard Robbins, late of Paris/San Diego, and Gudrun LaDoire, then of Paris, who introduced us to Western Europe when we moved to Neuilly-sur-Seine; with the many visitors who came to see Israel with us during the two semesters we lived in Haifa – my cousins Betty and Janet (Brodsky), the Clelands of Sedona, the Gazins of Hermosa Beach (who also went on the Egypt excursion with us and the Newbroughs) and the Brooks of Swampscott, MA. My cousin, Louis Burke, along with cousins Alyse and Nancy - nee Stern – who gathered with us at Louis' villa in Cap D'Antibes. We regret not mentioning the galaxy of other travel companions that we have inadvertently omitted.

OTHER BOOKS by Robert F. Brodsky
(see amazon.com/books)

On the Cutting Edge (Gordian Knot Books, 2006)

Songs My Mother Never Sang to Me (FOXBRO Press, 2008)

A Pilgrim Muddles Through (FOXBRO Press, 2009)

The World in a Jug (FOXBRO Press, 2010)

Catch a Rocket Plane (FOXBRO Press, 2012)

OTHER BOOKS BY FOXBRO PRESS
Bobby's World, by Bette Brodsky (2014)

CONTENTS

PREFACE

TROUBLE, RIGHT HERE IN RIVER CITY

This book, '*Pat and Bob TRIP the Light Fantastic*', my 6th and presumably last (since I am 89 as of May, 2014), was doomed from its inception. It is a hard luck book – and has only been completed and published chiefly for the benefit of our family and friends. The only positive side is that it turned out to be a good book, albeit missing several of our many journals because I do not have the strength or memory to try to reconstruct them. But, as it turned out, it will act as a good travel guide for trips to several overseas places that we have visited, or in which we lived, and people we befriended along the way.

The Tragedy (or Holocaust) came when the book was 98% finished and almost ready to email to the publisher. One day – early in March 2014 – a day that will live in author infamy - a big red 'RANSOM' note filled my computer screen and said, "***You have 3 days to pay us $400 or*** (so it said, as if they were equivalent) ***400 Euros or we will NOT de-encrypt all your WORD files***". I did NOT pay the ransom; instead choosing to invest $149.99 with each of 2 consecutive companies; both of whom said they could rid me of the virus and restore my files (and, alas, couldn't after many hours and days of working with them). Thus, the book was lost forever, along with everything else in WORD that was not in a 'zippered' file, and most of our picture library.

Very discouraged, I then forced myself into a long tedious recovery mode. I gradually found that some pertinent files were either available on a back-up 'stick' or had been put in a closed file which the virus apparently couldn't reach. In addition, I have been able to make some email attachment recoveries from the World Wide Web 'cloud', and from some available 'rough draft' hard copies that I could scan back into the computer. By these means and with considerable time-consuming grunt work on my computer, I was able to recover about 70% to 75% of the book, and decided to call it a day. Thus, it is a thin (and blood besmeared) book!

In mid-March, on a TV news broadcast, we heard that a woman <u>had</u> paid the ransom; got her files back; and 3 days later was again attacked. The story is that the virus came from Russia. Is this another cold war?

INTRODUCTION

Pat and I have been very fortunate in that our lives have included travel to many wonderful places all around the world. In this book, our purpose is NOT to describe them in exquisite detail, but rather to act as a travel guide. We will direct you to the sites that can be seen when you are traveling or living in the countries, cities, and bodies of water that fate has led us to. In what follows, "I" will be me, Bob; "She" will be my dear wife and many-time traveling companion, Pat (Patti, wife); and "we" will be the both of us.

Before we moved to Paris in 1969, neither of us had been out of the USA except for short forays into Mexico and Canada. Following our living in Paris in '69-'70, our serious travels began in 1975. In that year, I was a NATO Science Fellow and we traveled to Moscow and Baku in Russia; to Berlin and thence to France – chiefly Poitiers and Toulouse, with a wonderful side trip to the ancient walled city of Carcassonne. In the 80's, before I retired, I had a tacit sweetheart deal with my company, TRW. I could submit a technical paper to the International Astronautical Federation every other year and, if accepted, they would pay my freight. My papers were always accepted so, in turn, we traveled to Rome, Lausanne, Innsbruck and Vienna, always taking nice side trip vacations to assure coverage of Western Europe's great sights.

These wonderful trips were always taken on somebody else's money. On retirement, it was hard to break into the frame of mind that we might have to spend our own money if we wanted to continue seeing the world - which we did. We were eased into self-financing future travel in the beginning by taking advantage of two new opportunities: I began giving 3-day seminars on Remote Sensing (from space) Systems and continued doing this for the next ten years. My gigs were not only in the USA, but also in Turino, London, Paris and Munich. We used all of these as opportunities for extra excursions to visit our friends in Frankfurt, Heidelberg, Paris and Esslingen (near Stuttgart). Also, right after retirement from TRW (I did not retire from teaching at USC (the University of Southern California) until 1996), I applied for a fellowship to teach my Space Systems Design course for the Fall Semester, 1989-90, at the TECHNION (Israel Institute of Technology) in Haifa. This materialized, and we made the first of our many delightful subsequent visits to the old country, while renewing our acquaintance with a cousin who had first moved there in 1948 and whose husband also taught at the TECHNION.

But, in between and subsequent to these partially subsidized trips, we painfully learned that we were going to have to face up to traveling on our own money. Fairly early in the game, Pat started to make a daily log of our activities during these junkets, to amplify the documentation we obtained on our camcorder and camera. Her theory was that we would someday make a book out of the compiled and rewritten travelogues and the many pictures and brochures that came with them. This is the stuff of which this book was to be made of before the holocaust and why Pat is the co-author. We hoped that our kids and grandkids, at least, would be interested. So, Friends and Fellow Travelers - this is it – or what's left of it!

Chapter 1

A SKETCH OF OUR TRAVELS

I grew up in Philadelphia, and except for visits to NYC and a month every summer in Atlantic City and occasional vacations in Poland Springs, Maine, lived in a confined world. My WW2 US Navy experiences had me stationed in such life-threatening places as Ithaca/NewYork, Chicago/Navy Pier, Michigan City/Indiana, Gulfport/Mississippi, Brunswick/Maine, Falmouth on Cape Cod, Atlanta, Cape Canaveral, the Norfolk Naval Station, and the Philadelphia Naval Yard plus a brief stay - after the Germans had retreated - in Rabat/Port Lyautey in Maroc. After the war, while finishing my school work in Ithaca and New York City, the only travel I did was within the contiguous States while I was doing my thesis-associated work or looking for a job. However, starting in 1949, after I took my first 'real' non-teaching or non-horn playing job, my business - in Albuquerque – and (until 1956) prior marriage travel took me to Alice Springs in Australia; Oahu, Hawaii; the Marshall Islands in the South Pacific; and many U.S. cities for technical meetings and visiting/working at many NASA and commercial facilities.

Before we were married, Patti, born in Altoona and raised in Turtle Creek - a suburb of Pittsburgh - did little traveling. She and a girl friend made forays into New York City and Miami, and she moved to Southern California, along with several family members. We met in Claremont, CA. circa 1956 and married in 1959. After our honeymoon in Miami (emanating from Claremont) with stops in Philly and New

Orleans en-route), Pat and I didn't start traveling together until the late '60s, when we and our kids moved to Paris. Prior to that, we had never been to Europe, but thereafter made the majority of our trips together and visited Europe. Several times. Patti documented most of them in folders with her comments, and illustrated with many pictures. I often wrote summaries of our trips to send to our friends using Patti's log notes as a 'quote' or as a guide.

Before my retirement from industry in 1988 and from academia in 1996, our travels were, for the most part, 'company'- sponsored for me, with Pat tagging along at little extra cost since my employer picked up most of the tab. My work in atomic weaponry in Albuquerque not only took me to Los Alamos when it was a 'closed' city, but to many other cities that had large high-speed wind tunnels: Buffalo (Cornell Aero. Lab - in the winter - Ugh!), Dayton at Wright Field (USAF), Pasadena at JPL and Cal Tech, Virginia near Newport News at NASA/Langley, Dangerfield in Eastern Texas (Johns Hopkins U. - Applied Physics Lab), Inglewood near LAX (Douglas A/C), plus NASA facilities in Cleveland(Glenn Space Flight Center - SFC), DC (NASA Headquarters in D.C.) and Greenbelt, Maryland (Goddard SFC), Houston (Johnson SFC), Mountain View, CA. {NASA Ames-near San Jose) and Huntsville, Alabama (Marshall SFC). Also, on the business route were the White Sands Proving Grounds in New Mexico, the NASA Stennis rocket engine test facility in Bay St. Louis, MS. (near Gulfport}, the Kennedy Space Center on Cape Canaveral, as well as out-of-the-way places like Ft. Churchill on Hudson Bay in Canada, and a launch range (Kiruna) in the very northern part of Sweden, from which our sounding rockets could get a very good 'look' at the Aurora Borealis.

When we moved to Ames, Iowa to join academia on a full time basis - I did three things that opened the way for extensive travel in-country: I joined the ASEE (American Society for Engineering Education), the ASAE (American Society for Aerospace Education), and ADCA (the Aerospace Department Chairman's Association). The ASEE met during the summer at Universities in the U.S. and Canada. We usually drove to the meetings, carefully stopping along the way to see the great sights afforded in both countries. Thus, trips to the U. of Washington in Seattle and the U. of British Columbia in Vancouver got us to Mt. Rushmore, Glacier, Grand Tetons and Yellowstone National Parks; to Texas Tech (Lubbock) for ASEE, and Mississippi State and Corpus Christie for ADCA meetings; while summer vacation trips from Iowa to California got us to Carlsberg Caverns, White Sands (trailing our sail boat and asking the startled gate attendant, "Where's the beach"), the Petrified Forest and the Meteor Crater, and Grand Canyon; and Bryce and Zion National Parks on our way back.

We moved back to California in 1980 where we've been ever since, except for visiting professor stays, and the travel flood gates opened! We visited Europe many times. I made a deal with my boss at TRW that, if I had a paper accepted, I could go to an IAF (International Astronautical Federation) meeting every other year. Thus, we went on trips -stopping at appropriate nearby sites – to Italy, Switzerland, Austria (Vienna and Innsbruck), and Russia - Moscow and Baku. After I retired, we made three types of trips: One, where I gave 3-day technical seminars (London, Paris, Munich, Turino, Milano/Lago Maggiore, Haifa); Two, where we began cruising with friends and family; and Three, where we paid our way, such as the visit to Cousin Louis' villa at Cap D'Antibes on the Riviera near Nice, followed by a stay at Lago Lugano and the normal stops in Germany and France.

Later land, sea and river journeys took us to the Columbia River, Alaska, both coasts of South American (including a fabulous tour of Iguassu Falls), all along the Mexican Riviera (several times), down to its southern border as well as into the Gulf of Baja California and Mexico's famous Copper Canyon (a day trip by train from its Eastern shore), visited Europe several times, boated down the Danube (Donau) via Prague to Budapest, Serbia, Rumania and Bulgaria, ending at the Black Sea. Other trips took us to Puerto Rico and all the West Indies islands, again several times. Another trip was an exploration of the Baltic Sea, starting in Stockholm with stops in Helsinki, Finland, St. Petersburg, Russia, Talinn, Estonia and Copenhagen Denmark. Work and vacations also took us to Hawaii (Oahu and Maui) on 3 occasions. So, except for Australia (where I did have a quick business visit to Alice Springs in the 80s), we have pretty much seen the world — and intend to tell you about it in the following:

Chapter 2

'ROUND THE WORLD – SPRING '99

It all started in the late summer of '98, when my Haifa cousin Susan and her husband Dick told us that their beautiful talented daughter, Betsy, who lived in Jerusalem was engaged to be wed some time next May; probably at her sister's home in Be'ersheva. Without hesitation, we said we'd be there! Gradually, we began thinking about the trip. My dear wife, Patti, her curiosity whetted by having made a serious illustrated-by-hand-drawing study in elementary school, had always wanted to see the Taj Mahal. So, we started thinking in terms of going around the World, stopping to see the Taj either on the way to, or back from, the Old Country. In Israel, we would naturally make our headquarters in our old Haifa stomping grounds, and catch up on the many friends that we have made during out three previous stays there; two of them when I was a visiting professor at the Technion.

As the wedding date started sliding towards late May, it became apparent that for hot weather/monsoon-season reasons, we should make the circumnavigation by traveling Westwards. For Taj viewing in the full moon opportunities, a late April departure (actually April 29) was called for, with a one month stay in Israel planned. Naturally, on our way back, we would visit our friends in Germany and France, and our youngest son, Jeff, and his family in Swampscott, Massachusetts.

Our plans started to gel when the wedding date settled down to May 30 and Susan and Dick found an inexpensive apartment for us in the nice Mediterranean - looking Carmeliya neighborhood, not far from our previous mountain-top dwellings near the central Carmel section of Haifa. They said that the apartment could probably hold another couple under crowded conditions, should we have any guests. Under the duress of signing a lease now, we established May 6-June 6 for our Israel stay and built the rest of the trip around those dates.

Through the Travel Section of the LA Times, I got in touch with a San Francisco travel agency that specializes in round the world bookings, and with the help of an ace travel agent managed to establish an itinerary of Singapore (via Taipeh), New Delhi, Amman, Frankfurt, Paris (via high speed TGV- train of Tres Grande Vitesse- from Aachen to Paris; 350 miles in 3 hours!), Boston, and home for under $2000 per each! By using Royal Jordanian Airlines from Delhi to Frankfurt, we ostensibly saved $400 each over El Al prices - but as you will see there is more to this than meets the eye.

I went on the internet and found that there are two buses a day that make a Haifa / Amman and vice-versa traverse, but I could not find out where you got the bus in Amman. By e-mail, I asked Dick to find out more about the bus, giving him the name "Trust Transportation Co." of Nazareth. He wrote back the first of "There is no bus from Haifa to Amman" proclamations[1], but allowed that he did find a daily Tel Aviv - Amman bus, which obviously solved no problems. We then agreed that on arrival in Amman, I would call him at our mutual friend's house in Afula - near the Jordan border crossing at the King Hussein Bridge (over the river Jordan), and he and Susan would leave for the crossing - the same one we had used two years earlier on our jaunt to Petra (cited by Wikipedia as one "one the new 7 Wonders of the

1 See "*No Bus to Amman*" in last Chapter of "*A Pilgrim Muddles Through*" for details

World – a city built into the sides of an almost inaccessible canyon) and the Roman-ruins town of Jerash (on a par with Ephesus in Turkey and Bet She'an & Caesarea in Israel) - in time to meet us on the Israeli side of the border crossing.

Plans were made via e-mail for our stays and tours in Singapore and Delhi/Agra. We had invited our friends, Jack and Sue Cleland of Sedona, both devout Catholics, to visit us in Israel and get the fabulous Brodsky tour, to now include some previously neglected Christian holy sites. Then, we carefully planned the packing logistics; schlepping only two large bags with wheels; a smaller strap-on-to-larger-bag rolling bag containing toiletries and valuable papers which we would keep with us on the plane; my camcorder case; and Patti's purse, and a shoulder catch-all bag. The latter always carries special "water" bottles whose Vodka contents we used to "thin" the airlines' iced orange juice. Yea, verily, the veteran travelers were now ready to go on yet another, "This is our last big trip, we're just too old for all this nonsense!"

The flight to Singapore (which is just North of the Equator, and was very hot, but dry) on China Airlines, aided by our "water" supply and sleeping pills, was uneventful. We arrived there in early afternoon feeling pretty good despite having lost a day to the International Date Line (Would we ever get it back? At my age, everyday is important!). We arrived at our hotel, the International YMCA in the heart of the boutique area, and phoned the regional head of Hughes Communications at the suggestion of his California boss - a friend of ours - and were advised about the best use of our limited time there and the restaurants to try. The advice – which we followed assiduously - turned out to be just right!

It developed that English-speaking Singapore is an up-scale Hong Kong, populated chiefly by people of the Chinese persuasion, and is the biggest port in the world (as evidenced by the multitude of large ships standing by in the harbor area waiting for unloading accommodations). Our plan for the rest of the day was to visit Orchard Avenue - the local Fifth Avenue - and to see the famous Raffles Hotel, have dinner, and call it a day. Next day – Saturday - we would visit and explore Sentosa Island; and lastly take a city tour on Sunday before departing, shortly after midnight, for New Delhi.

Raffles, an easy walk from our hotel, had recently been refurbished back to its original British-Empire state of grandeur, and was indeed a grand old lady well reflective of the empire at its peak. We had the mandatory "Singapore Sling" at the Long Bar and found it to be insipid and cloying drink, hardly an antidote to the hot- around 90 degrees- but dry and therefore tolerable, climate. There is a mall-like area near our hotel called Chijmes, a remade monastery now comprising shops and many excellent ethnic restaurants, where we had our evening meal that night, and the two subsequent evenings.

The next day, we taxied to Mount Faber, and by a very high gondola ride over the harbor, arrived at Sentosa, Singapore's playground island. We took a slow open train which circled the island and noted the stops we wanted to make. Out of many options, we choose to visit an excellent nautical museum and an unusual aquarium (where a moving beltway took you through a glass-enclosed tunnel surrounded by great varieties of sea life whizzing over your head) and returned to the mainland by ferry (much like the famous ferry connecting Hong Kong to Kowloon). We had late lunch at a very authentic restaurant in Chinatown, and 'did' Orchard Road some more on our way back to the "Y". Before dinner, we had cocktails in the observation room of the highest (71 stories) hotel building in Asia - a Westin Hotel where you get a great view of the whole of Singapore.

The tour on Sunday covered some of the ground we had already seen - such as Chinatown and Mt. Faber- but emphasized what a lush, clean city/state Singapore is. We saw the old colonial part - replete with cricket club - the Parliament House, Supreme Court, and City Hall; drove through the Arabic and Little India sections; stopped at a resplendent Hindu temple (Sri Mariamman, the city's oldest, right next to Shakey's Pizza) which featured a tower with hundreds of beautiful colored carvings of figures and cattle, and ended up at the spectacular Orchid Gardens. We didn't realize that there were hundreds of varieties of the flowers - most being lovely. It was a fitting end to our visit.

Shortly after midnight, we embarked to New Delhi on Air India. We encountered a group of people who, according to an official, were traveling for the first time. Their "pushiness" exceeded the best native Israelis could do by far! But, we survived and arrived in New Delhi around 4 am, after a time zone change which was one and a half hours! (There are two such off-hour time zone changes in that mysterious part of the world, and it drives you crazy to find your watch inexplicably disagreeing with local time by a half hour). As scheduled, our driver-for-the-duration, an agreeable young man named Pankage was there, replete with a sign to assure our meeting. He subsequently proved himself to be driver with nerves of steel; in a place where such nerves were continually called upon. He understood English perfectly but seemed loathe to speak it in any but basic forms. We immediately felt the high and humid heat. It never fell below 100 degrees while we were there, and reached 115 in mid afternoon. We never saw a blue sky; the sky was white with the Indian summer brand of smog which only the monsoons wipe away, apparently.

We were delivered to our Delhi headquarters, the India International Centre, located in the midst of diplomatic row. Our stay there was arranged by the father of a former student of mine, now a friend, Madhu Thangevelu. His father, Dr.

Thangevelu – just deceased in 2009, was employed by the World Health Organization and was a member of the Centre, thus – through his intervention - making us eligible to stay in this lovely hostel-like convention center where people meet to discuss solutions to India's many problems. The compound included about 40 two-room suites, many meeting rooms, a dining room and a bar; all in a sylvan setting adjacent to large park. Madhu says he remembers staying there with his family (his Father lived in Bombay, now Mumbai) and romping around the fields with his brothers and sisters. It also houses a travel agency that arranged for all our excursions in India. We moved in, had breakfast, watched CNN, napped a bit and set out on our 11 a.m. city tour; Pankage and our guide, Jimmy, having arrived precisely on time to pick us up.

Unlike Singapore, a city replete with high rise buildings and an approximately equal 4 million population, New Delhi's highest building might be a 6-8 story apartment house. Except for Old Delhi, and the incongruous cows which wander unfettered through the streets, it is a typical sprawling metropolis with a few outstanding sites. We saw the "India Gate", a huge Arc de Triomph-like WW I war memorial, the Parliament houses and adjacent President's palace, arranged as a U, with an impressive mall leading to the India Gate about a quarter of a mile away. We had lunch with our guide, an erudite educated man who opined that India's vast problems would never be solved by the succession of crooked politicians who were and had been running the country. We proceeded to Lakshmi Narayan Hindu temple, where we were blessed by a Monk who bedecked us with flowers and put a red spot on our foreheads (As you will see, the blessing didn't take); went to the famous "Red" fort where Shah Jehan, the builder of the Taj, moved the government after a severe water shortage in Fatepur Sikri; drove through Old Delhi and called it a day; retiring early to be ready for our early morning pick-up for Agra and the Taj Mahal, and then nearby Fatepur Sikri.

We marveled at Pankage's driving skill as he negotiated the hazards of the suburban towns of Delhi, fending his way through heavy auto traffic in a very nice sedan is produced in India and is ubiquitous (you seldom see foreign makes, except in the diplomatic/governmental areas). In addition to cars, he dealt with bicycles, bicycle taxis, tractors, camels, donkeys, an occasional laden elephant, hordes of gaily clad pedestrians, and the ever present cattle. We also got our first look at the abject poverty that abounds in India - but nothing like we would see later. Eventually, we got to a semi-freeway, and uneventfully arrived in Agra, a bustling medium-sized city, about 110 miles away. About halfway there, we had stopped for lunch, being careful, as always in India, to drink beer or bottled water. Madhu had warned us of the dreaded "Delhi Belly", whose revenge is considered much worse than Montezuma's, even if Pepto Bismal is administered liberally. (For trip preparation, we had taken Malaria pills, and were given booster Tetanus shots, but not Hepatitis 'A' shots, as our doctor thought they would not be necessary in such a short trip, so long as we didn't bathe in the Ganges, or the like).

We stayed at the new Trident Hotel - an oasis insulated from the grim realities of Mother India - located near, but not in sight of the Taj. Almost immediately, our new local guide called us, rarin' to go. We cooled him by saying we wanted to have a leisurely lunch before starting on our tour of Agra. This apparently ticked him off and he remained somewhat surly throughout - the complete antithesis of Jimmy.

We were picked up at 2 pm, and went to Agra Fort, in which Shah Jehan had a palace where his entourage occasionally stayed while the Taj was being erected, and where he spent the last of his life under house arrest - deposed by his oldest son. But at least it was least in view of the Taj, where his dear wife, Mumtaz Mahal, (and later, himselff) was entombed. The temperature in the fort was a mere 115 degrees and the visit was tortuous. We did get our first look at the Taj, a distance away and obscured by the smog. The glimpse only whetted our appetite. Much to our guide's chagrin, we then asked to return to the hotel, to be picked up later to see the Taj, for the first time, at sunset.

What can you say about the Taj Mahal, after you say it's magnificent! As the sinking sun grayed the normal completely white Indian sky, the white marble took on subtle shades of blue, and the natural beauty of the structure was further enhanced. We had arrived there from the parking lot a quarter of a mile away via a crazy contraption powered by a motorcycle engine. It carried four comfortably, but we saw some with two extra people hanging on to the side The entry gate was in the middle of a high walled structure that surrounded the Taj on three sides - the rear side faced onto the now dry river bed. Our surly guide bought us entry tickets, and collected the rupees from me (not cricket according to our agreement with the travel company) and then shortchanged us! I chose not to call him on it.

As we entered, we almost gasped at the shear beauty of the site- the gorgeous mosque with the long reflecting pool leading up to it made the whole trip an instant success! Only pictures can do justice to the site if you cannot see it in person - and we have plenty of them! I took camcorder pictures from the entry way, but had to check it before going further (still cameras were not banned). We were almost immediately accosted by a professional cameraman who offered to take pictures of us at a dollar each. We said we would try a few, and he and his aide immediately took charge of posing us innumerable times. We ended up buying a booklet at $40 - the best investment we've ever made as it turned out.

When we finally got a chance to see the Taj unescorted, the sun was starting to go down and some of the magic we expected was beginning to happen. Patti used her throw-a-way camera to record the scene. We soon were approached by a gentleman who said he was only a humble gardener here, but could show us the best views to take sunset pictures. He rushed us from one spot to another, pointing and saying, "here". At the end, I thanked him profusely and offered him what I thought was a nice tip of $2.00. He nastily scorned this, and I ended up paying $5. Scammed again – humble gardener indeed! As we left, we found that due to a terrorist threat a few months ago, the Taj was no longer open on full moon nights - and there is no good way to see it in moonlight due to the surrounding wall. We did buy a beautiful moonlight shot postcard - some compensation? Thus fell a major reason for planning our trip the way we did.

As we went back to the hotel, we discussed tomorrow's activities. We wanted to see the Taj at sunrise, return to the hotel for breakfast and checkout, and the go to Fatepur Sikri before returning to Delhi. The guide started to persuade us that his services were not really necessary in Fatepur Sikri -we could hire a local guide there that he would pay for - and we cheerfully agreed. The Taj at sunrise presents a different, but equally sensational aspect. The color shades and shadows give another breathtaking view. We drank it in and proceeded to Fatepur Sikri, about 12 miles away, East towards Jaipur (which people tell us is also a worthwhile stop). Pankage found us a guide, a weathered old man - older than me! - cloaked in robes and sporting a gold tooth. He was very knowledgeable and had much enthusiasm for the very impressive fort that once was the seat of the Indian government under Shah Jehan. We entered through the 175 foot high gateway that guards the Fort. The insides were very impressive - more so than the Agra Fort and the Red Fort in Delhi. The royal quarters were spacious and – for the fifteen hundreds when they were abandoned- looked to be comfortable. It was also very hot - we had to tell the guide to stop and rest quite a few times (he remained gung-ho!) and was disappointed when, exhausted, we declined to see the whole shebang.

Since we did not have to take the surly guide back to Agra, Pankage elected to return to Delhi via a supposed "shortcut" through the back roads with which he was not familiar. As uncomfortable as the trip was (it was very hot despite the car's air conditioning and we were hungry; we lost our way several times; and later badly needed a pit stop which never materialized, we were glad we had endured the three hour ordeal- for we saw the "real" India. The "real" India is not a sight you really want to see. The poverty, filth, and chaos we saw (e.g., children sharing water holes with herds of pigs, while clothes "washing" was going on) along the way was unbelievable. Many people were homeless and many appeared without hope. We saw no evidence of schools or outhouses. The little villages were jammed with humanity and frail living structures. Even the fields looked starved. We immediately lost our taste to ever go to India again.

After wandering 40 years in the desert, we finally got back on the freeway and stopped to eat at the same place as on our way down to Agra. As soon as we arrived at the Centre, Patti made us drinks, using ice cubes from our suite's refrigerator – which proved to be a bad mistake. We had dinner and went to bed early, since Pankage would pick us up at 3:00 am to go to the airport for our flight to Jordan. The dreaded "Delhi Belly" hit us both at about 1:00 am, but only - so far – lightly. Its full vengeance was not to be wreaked until just before breakfast was being served on the Royal Jordanian Airlines on the way to Amman. My stomach felt queasy, and I asked for tea. Despite this, I was turning white as a sheet. Suddenly, I knew I had to get to the bathroom, but before I could raise the tray, I vomited all over the place! The chief flight attendant hurried over - she said she knew I was in distress earlier - and cleaned up what she could. I think I set back the mid-east "Peace Process" (in Israel, they pronounce it "Piss", and I have never been sure whether it is an accent or a social commentary) a few years. I cleaned up as best I could, but did feel much better. But I had to sit another 4 hours in soiled, smelly clothes, which I'm sure pleased our fellow passengers no end. On to Jordan!

We had been in Jordan previously (see Chapter 7, *Israel/ Jordan*): On one of our visits to Haifa in 1998, we took a very interesting side trip to Amman; using our hotel there as a base for guided tours of the built-into-a-rock-cliff city of *Petra* and the Roman-ruins city, *Jerash*. We were joined by cousin Susan, her husband Dick, and friends of theirs, the Abelson's, from *Afula*, an Israeli city near the Jordan border. Each excursion took a day, and was well worth the time and effort. At that time, I could still walk distances fairly well and could keep up with our entourage.

We arrived in Amman at 9:30 am local time, readjusted our wrist watches for the crazy half hour bit (little did we know that Jordan was on standard time, while Israel was on daylight time) and, with some difficulty but armed with Dinars that I had purchased in India), made the call to Afula to inform our cousins of our arrival and intent to get a taxi to the King Hussein Bridge crossing. We carefully told the taxi driver our where we wanted to go and felt sure that he understood. On the way out of the airport, he showed us the only airport hotel, the *Alia*, and we discussed staying there the night before our early Sunday morning departure to Frankfurt at the end of our stay in Haifa.

The drive to the crossing seemed longer that we remembered from two years ago, but the border station and procedures seemed and looked the same. When, after an hour of customs hi-jinks on both sides, we arrived safely on the Israel side, we wondered where cousins Susan and Dick were. I took the opportunity to change into clean clothes. We waited and waited and were just about to call Afula when we were tapped on the shoulder and asked if we were "The Brodsky's"? It turned out that the wicked taxi driver had taken us to the Allenby Bridge crossing; the one people going to Jerusalem use. It was some 60 miles south of the King Hussein crossing where our cousins awaited. A scary $100 along the Arab-populated West Bank taxi ride and two hours later, we were in Afula and reunited with our family and friends, but the savings over *EL AL* travel were already being seriously eaten into. Our one month stay in the Old Country now began, but the ravages of the Delhi belly would continue for the next few days.

On our way to our Haifa apartment, Susan and Dick told us that they were having some stress. A few days before our arrival, their daughter had called them to say that the wedding was off! Then, next day, it was on again - but they were still biting their nails. In one week from then, next Thursday, the first big wedding event was scheduled. It was to be a party in Haifa giving their friends an opportunity to meet the prospective bridegroom, and to bring wedding presents - since the wedding was to be in Be'ersheva. This was to be followed by a Saturday night fete for their congregation at their nearby Shul. Their uneasiness was enhanced by the forthcoming arrival of two of their sons with their wives, a granddaughter, and Dick's sister; all coming from the States. They had also made extensive plans in Be'ersheva for a rehearsal dinner, an all day guided bus tour to Masada, followed by the wedding and banquet. In addition, they helped their daughter with her wedding gown and other generous pre-nuptial gifts. All this in the face of Dick's imminent retirement from teaching at the Technion.

As soon as we entered our new rental apartment, we could see that although it would be great for us for a month, there was no way that Susie and Jack could fit in. There was a living room with a fold-out couch, a bedroom of good size, and the craziest combination kitchen-bathroom that you ever saw! In two days, our friendship would have been a shambles. So, we asked cousin Susan to look for a rental place while we checked out local hotels. All of the latter were over $120/night, but Susan found a beautiful apartment for half the price, whose availability fit the Cleland's travel plans. We went to see it, and it was super - much nicer than our apartment, with a panoramic harbor view all the way to the Lebanese border. We grabbed it and proceeded to reacquaint ourselves with our Haifa friends and the beach. That Monday, revisiting the Technion, I gave my invited lecture on 'Resolution from Space' to a wildly appreciative crowd that shouted "huzzah" (or, Oy Veh! I forget which) and carried me off on their shoulders.

Before our Arizona friend's arrival, I decided to plan how we would get back to the Amman airport for our Sunday, June 6 flight to Frankfurt. It seemed obvious that there was no way to leave Haifa very early on Sunday with any hope of making a 9 am plane, especially if this was an hour earlier Israel time and the border crossing did not open until 7 am. It was also worrisome about traveling to Jordan on Saturday, since Israel pretty much closes down public transportation on the Sabbath. I went to a travel agency to buy a ticket for the bus between Haifa and Amman and to make a reservation for Saturday night at the *Alia* Hotel at the Amman airport, which is a good 25 miles from greater downtown Amman. After considerable rummaging around on the computer, I was told in no uncertain terms that, "There is no bus to Amman" (confirming Dick's earlier pronouncement) and "There is no *Alia* Hotel"! It became immediately apparent that the tenuous "piss" agreement between Jordan and Israel had not really taken hold. Back at home, I called the Trust Transportation number in Nazareth which I had taken from the internet, and was assured that there were two buses daily from Haifa to Amman, and was told where to get a ticket in the harbor area of Haifa.

Susie and Jack arrived on Wednesday, the day before the big pre-wedding party. They had missed Lufthansa connections in Chicago and arrived at Ben Gurion over 5 hours late and without luggage. Before we took them to their apartment, we showed them ours - so that they would see why staying with us was impossible. We had a guilty conscience, since they did not anticipate the extra expense, but they loved their place and their landlord Zvi, a real Israeli old timer, continuously regaled them with sea stories about the beginnings of the country. Alas, it would be exactly one (!) unbelievable week before their bags showed up! The airline allowed them to spend $100 each on clothes- and they managed by doing a lot of laundry and clothes borrowing. Both deserve "Hero of the Soviet Union" awards!

The next evening, after having given up for today on what would be a daily luggage vigil, we arrived in the lobby of our cousin's apartment for the big introductory party, wedding present in hand. Right then and there, we should have suspected the worse. I pushed the door bell and nothing happened! We had to wait until a resident came along to open the door before we could enter.

We finally met the groom, an Englishman, a fiftyish sociology professor and musician (clarinet and soprano sax) face-to-face. I had been communicating with him by e-mail because of our mutual interest in traditional jazz and his consummate interest in some of my rare Sidney Bechet records. In person, he was likeable and voluble. He confirmed that he had bought a house in Roq Brun, near Beziers in southeast France where they would live for most of the year, and that his two daughters - from his previous marriage - and his mother were all coming from Old Blighty for the wedding. He also played me a few choruses on his clarinet - but not enough for me to truly judge his prowess. He said he had been living with his bride-to-be in her Jerusalem apartment for about a month - the longest continuous exposure to each other in their one year courtship. We next joyfully talked at length with her, and heard her express her trepidation at leaving her family and friends in Israel for a new country - although she does speak French avec some fluency. She said she hoped that they would live some part of the year in Jerusalem and, to this end, had not put her apartment on the market. She also noted that her man was not enthralled with her flute playing; and hoped he would relent in his insistence that her dog, Jake, now 13, be an "outdoors-only" pet in Roq Brun.

That night, staying at our cousin's place, the bride and groom had a serious argument that was soothed by Susan and Dick; but after the successful reception at the Shul on Saturday, Susan found her daughter curled up on their living room sofa at 2 am. Her first words were, "I'm not going through with it!", recounting the many reasons for her decision. At some point, the groom emerged from the bedroom, and was told the news. She told him she was not returning to Jerusalem with him. He tried to dissuade her, but was politely asked to leave. They fed him breakfast and he took off for Jerusalem and returned to England. Could this marriage be saved? Nobody on our side thought so, and even she seemed somewhat relieved.

Now began the many calls to the party attendees to give them the news and to the USA to sons, sister, and granddaughter to inform them that the wedding was cancelled. All said they would come anyway to show family support. The Be'ersheva activities would go on as planned

only sans the Groom! But, our cousins' tribulations were not yet over. One by one, starting with the doorbell, and in the midst of their sons' arrivals, their kitchen range failed and had to be replaced; their dishwasher failed and required a hard-to-find part; their car was broken into and though not stolen, had its wiring ripped to shreds; and – tragically- their great granddaughter - a lovely red-headed 11 year old - was diagnosed with a severe case of anorexia. Dick said to me, "And you think Job had troubles?"

Jaffa-Tel Aviv – Old and New

During Susie and Jack's 12 day visit, we saw almost everything in Israel that a visitor should see, except Eilat on the Red Sea in the deep south, and Jaffa/ Tel Aviv (due to a luggage arrival time-out). We hit the beaches and great sights in Haifa (the B'Hai Temple, the Carmelite Nunnery and Monastery, the Sculpture Garden, the Clandestine Museum - where Dick is pictured as one of the founders

of the Israeli Navy in 1949 -; the Technion campus (it is the MIT of Israel); rode the *Carmelit*, Israel's only subway, which connects Carmel with the harbor waterfront area; the Turkish market there; the artist's colony at Ein Hod, and the nearby Druze villages. We made day trips to Acco (Acre) with its wonderful ancient harbor and long winding colorful souk (Casbah); Rosh Ha'niqra at the Lebanese border with its beautiful grottos which rival the Blue Grotto at Capri; Caesarea, replete with its Roman amphitheater and harbor and Crusader castles, and also found time to celebrate my 74th at a dinner at Susie's place, with Susan and Dick as guests. We also celebrated Barak's lopsided victory over Bibi Netanyahou, which pleased our local friends no end.

HAIFA – HOME OF THE B'HAI FAITH AND TOMB OF THE B'AB

We then began the Christian part of the tour, starting with a day trip to Nazareth to visit the church of the Annunciation, where Mary's pregnancy was announced, to the Jordan River site where Jesus was baptized and to Mt. Tabor to visit the Church of the Transfiguration, which marks the site where God announced that Jesus was his son. I tend to take these happenings at face value.

During the period we were hanging around Haifa waiting for the luggage, we combined our ride downtown on the *Carmelit* with a quest for Amman bus tickets. We easily found the travel agency where I was told I could get the tickets, but they advised me to walk "200 meters down Ha'Atzma Ut (Avenue of Independence)" and look for the terminal near the entry to the Port. We did so, but found no bus terminal. I went into a travel agency right across from the port entry and asked where I could but a ticket for the bus to Amman. They immediately said, "There is no bus to Amman", and I decided to try again after Jack and Susie left. As for a hotel reservation, there was better news. I asked our landlady, Mrs. Shindler (no relation) if she could help and she directed me to her "wonderful" agent (Ordinarily, Dick's travel agent, who had done us proud on our Jordan trip two years ago probably would have been able to solve our problem but, alas, he had recently died in the course of duty in Albania). A few days later, we got a call from our new agent, who proudly told us that while there was no hotel *Alia*, she did book us into a hotel "near the airport which had the airport shuttle service" that we had insisted on. I was temporarily placated and elated.

We next started off on our grand tour of the Old Country, for which the Brodsky's became justly noted. First, at the start of a blistering heat wave reminiscent of India, we drove to the ancient mystical town of Zefat (Safed), which was absolutely dead, since it was Saturday. We saw what we could, especially two very old synagogues and the bullet-ridden police building which had been the center of the fight which 'liberated' Zefat. After lunch, we visited the war memorial in the Golan Heights, and ended the day by checking into the Scottish Mission in Tiberias, an old stamping ground and our home for two nights in the Sea of Galilee area.

The next day, we started off at the kibbutz Ginnosar, with its wonderful museum and ancient recovered boat; then on to the Mount of Beatitudes where Jesus gave the Sermon on the Mount. We drove higher for a lunch stop at the dude ranch, Vered Ha'galil (Rose of Galilee), where Walter Cronkhite used to hang out during the Syrian war, and then back to the Sea to visit Tagpha, where Jesus performed the miracle of the loaves and fishes, and then to Capernaum, where Jesus met and baptized Peter, the Big Fisherman, and had an early synagogue. Before we called it a day, we went looking for the creaky old bridge across the Jordan River which used to separate Israel from Jordan, but missed it. A new bridge had taken its place. We did find the old one, now blocked off to traffic, and wondered how the wretched old one lane structure had withstood the ravages of time so long.

The next morning, we set off with Jerusalem as our ultimate destiny. We had intended to go to Hamat Gader, the site of fabulous Roman baths and a huge alligator farm, but our companions wanted to see Yardenit, the serene place where Jesus was purportedly baptized. It is located where the Jordan flows south out of the Sea of Galilee towards its ultimate destiny - the Dead Sea, and it indeed proved to be very peaceful. Because of the heat and the hour, we decide to forego Hamat Gader and instead headed to Bet She'an, a marvelous world class (aye, the equal or better than Ephesus in Turkey and Jerash in Jordan) Roman

city relic, still being dug out. The temperature on its main street was 110 degrees! From there, we headed smack dab through the West Bank quite uneventfully to Big J, albeit the road skirted Little J (Jericho). By sheer luck - since we had never entered Jerusalem from this direction- we found our hotel at the Hebrew Union College, hard by the walls of the Old City, without any trouble. Strike up one for the pure of heart!

THE ROMAN BATHS AT HAMAT GADER

That evening we walked to the famous Ben Jehuda area with all its indoor and outdoor restaurants. We saw the beautiful lighted walls of the old city from our rooms, and so to bed over the din of a wedding party going on at the patio below. Our first venture in Big J was what we recommend for all visitors - take Bus 99, which picks you up near the King David Hotel (which is a stone's throw from the Hebrew Union). This is an inexpensive, English-narrated 2 plus hour tour which takes you to past all the city's highlights. It thus allows you to decide which places you want to see in more detail. After lunch, we entered the Old City via the Jaffa Gate, and headed immediately through the Moslem Quarter to the Christian Quarter and the Church of the Holy Sepulchre, which encompasses the grounds on which Christ was crucified and buried. We hired an Arab guide to take us through the church, since here, for once, I cannot claim to be expert in things of the spirit. Susie and Jack were appalled by the crass commercialism in this most holy area, and were shocked to find several "Stations of the Cross" on Via Dolorosa partially covered by vendor's blankets and/or "T" shirts. We met 'the 'Bride' and Susan's newly arrived granddaughter, (their Kentucky son's – Dick and Susan's oldest son - daughter) for dinner, and found the 'Bride' in good spirits and only a little shell shocked. Before retiring, we had drinks in the lobby of the King David- another "must" for visitors - since it gives you the ambiance of rubbing shoulders with the world's big shots. Over drinks, Patti and I discussed whether we should send Cousin Dick a bill for the new wedding outfits we had both bought, but the Cleland's dissuaded us for the nonce. I had even bought a tie, despite my solemn vow never to wear one again after retirement!

The next morning, we met the granddaughter and went on a guided tour of the Old City, visiting the Jewish quarter and the Wailing Wall and the ancient Roman Cardo, the Armenian and Moslem quarters, and ending up in the Christian quarter, redoing the Church of the Holy Sepulchre under, this time, our Jewish guide's interpretations. We had lunch near the Jaffa Gate, and Patti and I left for Haifa, leaving the Cleland's to do Masada and Bethlehem on their last two days.

JERUSALEM – THE WAILING WALL IN THE 'OLD CITY'

We had a few days left to do gift shopping, socialize with old friends, hit the beach, and once more try to buy bus tickets to Amman before the big Be'ersheva bash. On Friday, May 28, we caravanned with Dick and Susan to the Be'ersheva Hilton Hotel in time to make Shabbat dinner at their eldest daughter's place in Omer, a suburb. Here, for the first time we met the members of their family that we did not yet know: The middle son, a research doctor of veterinary medicine in Connecticut, and his wife, and their oldest son, then the well-known manager of Three Chimneys horse farm- which features Seattle Slew at stud, among others-, and his lady friend both from Versailles (pronounced "Versals", to the chagrin of Francophiles worldwide), Kentucky. The entire original wedding party - except the aforementioned groom - was present at the dinner/reception -; all of Dick's and Susan's children except their youngest, Portland, Oregon, son and his family, were there; plus grandchildren and great-great grandchildren! It was fun meeting the "new" family members. The oldest son, who had recently obtained a "Kentucky Colonelship" for Dick, lives near an old Navy buddy of mine, and I resolved to visit him and my other friends in the vicinity (my last college roomie, Dick Allen, lives in nearby Cinncy, along with another Cornell buddy). I busily documented the whole group with my camcorder, using this unprecedented opportunity to the utmost. Alas, the Friday night before leaving Israel, I inadvertently and stupidly left the damn thing in the taxicab that took us from Susan and Dick's to our apartment (we had turned in our rental car earlier in the day, and Dick cannot drive on Shabbat). Thus disappeared the entire visual documentation of the trip, although Susie and Jack got a lot of film on their camcorder during our tour which they subsequently shared with us.

We returned to Haifa the next day, not wishing to go on the Masada trek that we had done several times in previous visits. Our last few days in Israel were spent seeing friends, going to the beach, seeing Susan and Dick when they were not showing their oldest son around, and doing more shopping at the Druze villages. On Thursday evening after dinner in central Carmel, I stopped at the taxi dispatch stand to arrange for an early Saturday morning pickup to take us downtown to get the bus to Amman. When I told the dispatcher the plan, he naturally said, "There is no bus to Amman", and, "No buses run on Saturday". I thanked him for the information and asked him to humor me. We spent our last evening at Dick and Susan's with their son and his lady, and then called for the fateful cab, whose driver, I feel sure, now has a nice camcorder to play with.

The bus ride to Amman was pleasant and uneventful, although it took over an hour to go through the King Hussein Bridge border crossing, and we were inexplicably charged $15 each to leave Israel! We were let off in downtown Amman and immediately transferred to a cab to go to the Airport hotel, or so we thought. About ten minutes later, the cabbie left us off at the downtown Amman hotel that I recognized we had stayed at two years prior on our way to Petra. I said that there must be some mistake because Mrs. Shindler's travel agent had promised us differently. I went to the desk and asked if they had shuttle bus service to the airport. "Of course", said the pretty clerk, "the taxis run all the time". Really teed off, I asked the Clerk if she would release us from our reservation and call the *Alia* for us. This was done, and we got to the *Alia* an hour later with not enough Dinars to pay the cab driver. He drove me to the nearby airport and a local ATM. After a pleasant evening and a great meal at the *Alia*, we were off to Frankfurt the next morning, with three weeks still left on our journey around the world.

Since we have always used Frankfurt as a jumping off place in Germany, we normally take the E-Bahn subway to the HofBahnHof to get the train to Stuttgart / Esslingen to see our dear friend Gretel. And this time, schlepping our bags through the underground maze, we arrived at the main station about an hour before our scheduled departure. We reveled at this- for one of our favorite doings has always been to go to a favorite Stand and get a Bratwurst sandwich and a stein of beer, which we absorb at a table watching the hurrying crowd go by. As fast as we could, we rushed to the Stand, only to find it had been displaced by a McDonald's (at the other former rival stand was a Burger King!). Later, we found that the Americanization of Europe had extended with equal evil to other sectors. The TRAINS no longer run exactly on time! We settled for a Restaurant in the station for the Bratwurst fix- but, not being available as a sandwich - it was just not the same. We boarded the train and soon found that the first stop- as of a week ago- was the Frankfurt airport! You remember the WW II movie about the Remagen Bridge, *"A Bridge Too Far"*? Well, we had endured in vain a "Schlep Too Far"! Live and learn!

Our week's stay with Gretel in Esslingen, a lovely suburb of Stuttgart, was pleasant as usual. We stayed in a guest house, die *Blauer Bock* (Blue Ram), a few steps from her condo. The time went quickly, visiting with Gretel's daughter, Betty, and her 93 year old mother, Oma, and her other family members whom we have known for years. We did little sightseeing, for we have covered most of the surrounding state in past visits. One day, however, we did see an outstanding condo community in nearby Plochingen. It was designed by a famous architect/artist named Hundertwasser, and it is one of five similar communities in Germany and Austria. There must be about 40 adjoining townhouse - type units, each unique, constructed in a triangular plot with the colorful house fronts facing the large garden - like triangular interior courtyard. A high fanciful tower is in the center of one of the three legs. It, like all the other houses, has a multicolored Daliesque finish and is topped out by golden spheres. Each interior - facing house is similarly outlandishly bedecked and every window is of a different size and shape. Balconies have trees growing on them. We decided that it would definitely be a fun place to live!

We left by train on Friday to Aachen. On the way, we made a three hour stop in Heidelberg to see and have lunch with our old friends Max and Nieta Klager. He's a Professor (of Pedagogie) at good old H.U. and she's the wife he met while he was getting his Ph.D at the U of Minnesota, and who now asks him in Deutsche, "Max, what's the English word for ----------?" Max is an author of books on art, which he usually translates into English, and is noted for his championing of the art produced by Down's Syndrome artists- vivid, bursting with color, and tres outre! Then, we were back on the train to Aachen, riding along the very picturesque Rhine River wine and castle country. It was here that we discovered the awful truth of train systems that are now privatized. We missed out connection at Cologne for Aachen - a heretofore unheard of happening! We boarded the next one a half hour later.

Finally arriving, we were greeted by Joachim (Yochen) Damm, the husband of my former German pen pal, Gudrun. We first met at the Apfelwein Restaurant in Neu Isenburg, near the Frankfurt airport, many years ago. I agreed then to write her in German, while she wrote to me in English- though she was always more competent than I. We mailed the corrections back and forth. At our first meeting, we conversed in our then only common language - French. When we met, Gudrun was studying to be a Judge - a position she later reached. Now, since they moved out of her probationary jurisdiction, and now have two children, she can no longer be a Judge without going through the apprenticeship process. So, temporarily at least, she is a lawyer (Avocat), generally working in medicine-related law, out of her home. Yochen is the financial director of Ericsson's German bureau. It is interesting to note that this giant Swedish communications company does all its business in English. What with the

Euro then being approximately the same value as the Dollar, and with English rapidly becoming the mutual European language (except, of course, in France), it was not hard to visualize a United States of Europe before too long, hastened by the new frenzy of conglomeration (viz, Chrysler/ Daimler-Benz).

Our adopted grandchildren, Marina (10) and Peter (7) greeted us like we had never been away! It was over three years. Mein Deutsche still gave them a lot of trouble - but Marina will start taking English in the Fall - and we promised to become pen pals. We visited downtown Aachen and Charlemagne's cathedral in the morning, and went to a very busy fair, in the suburbs, in the afternoon. The children had a ball - with rides and junk food! We ate at a fine restaurant - all in all a lovely day with our "kids". Gudrun and Yochen honeymooned with us in Hermosa Beach; visited us a few years ago, and next (Fall, 2001) will bring Die Kinder (we promised them Disneyland and Universal City).

We took the TGV to Paris - 350 miles in 3 hours! - on Sunday morning and were met at Gare Du Nord by Les Ladoires; Gudrun (another one) and Claude. Gudrun was the office manager when I was Aerojet's "Manager of European Operations" in the late 60's. She was then the brains of the gang and kept me out of trouble. She handles French, English, German, and Spanish with equal facility. Claude's English is not good, and it took a few hours for my French to come back with any fluency. I couldn't stop sprechening die Deutsche! At the station, I cashed in my leftover D-Marks for Francs, but for some reason they could not give me money with my VISA card. I was directed to an ATM, and here began a comedy of errors - still inexplicable - which led me to go from one ATM to another - each time being allowed to take out 200-300 Francs (about $35 - $50) each transaction! After we left our bags off at our hotel, we drove about 50 miles in the direction of Lyon towards their retirement compound in Cudot (they had recently given up their pied-a-terre in Paris), stopping along the way at ATMs. Cudot is on the edge of the Burgundy region and is absolutely serene and sylvan in nature. They have a lovely place with two houses and lots of lawn and flower beds and a great miniature Schnauzer, "*Jazz*". Cudot is a small isolated village- about 10 houses- which abuts large fields and pastures. It is truly idyllic! That evening, Claude cooked great steaks on a fireplace grill while we reminisced about the old days. Next morning, we drove to the rail station in a lovely old town, Sens, where we roamed through the pedestrian mall and had lunch before boarding the train back to Paris.

We took the Metro from the Gare de l'Est to the stop next to our hotel. For the second consecutive time, we had chosen to stay in the Hotel of the City Hospital (Hospitel), which is maintained for the benefit of aus-landers coming to visit hospital patients. The glorious thing about it, besides the modest $80/night - with breakfast - cost, is that it is smack dab next door to Notre Dame, and right at the start of the Boul'Mich action. It is well appointed and comes with a night key for use when the hospital lobby entry is closed. The last time we were there, we turned in the key at the hotel desk, as we hurried to make a very early train to the airport. The lobby was closed, and we couldn't find our way out of the hospital! I was so panicked that I lost all my French, and the people thought I wanted to be admitted. This time, we were forewarned. When we arrived at the hotel desk, we found a message from our old navy friend, Tommy Carrig, who now lives in Copenhagen. Despite the fact that he had had a stroke several months ago, we had hoped he and his wife Nancy would join us in Paris- but the note canceling the reservation we had made for them said, "No".

That night, we made our first pilgrimage to our favorite restaurant "*L'Entrecote*", also known as "*Les Relais de Venise*", just off of the Pt. Maillot stop of Metro #1 line. Our mouth watering was not in vain - the standard and only fare - steak (saignant-rare) with the fabulous mustard sauce, les pommes-frites, the walnut salad and the red house wine were, as usual, magnificent! After dinner, we walked to our old Monoprix super market to buy some liquid 'supplies'. On the Metro back, we both agreed that it was great to be back in Paris, where we had lived in 1969-70.

The bells of Notre Dame - a stone's throw from our window - woke us up next morning. After petit dejeuner in our room, we Metroed to Le Bourget to see the Paris Air Show; my first appearance there since June, 1969! The big difference the intervening years made was the appearance of booths, companies, and exhibits dealing with things spacial, where before it had been almost exclusively things aeronautical. Nevertheless, I was amazed at the huge variety of aircraft that were exhibited from an equally huge number of countries. The fly-bys - generally on ten minute centers - were both ear busting and daring: Airplanes going straight up; Helicopters doing loops, and, the day before so we were told, a Russian aircraft barreling in with its two pilots safely ejecting just before hitting the ground. We visited the Aerojet booth and I met the man who was now their European Manager - but his job, selling- was much different than mine was 30 years ago. We also visited the Launchspace booth looking for its president and old friend, Marshall Kaplan (He has sponsored my seminars on Remote Sensing Systems in the US and abroad). We left him a note to have dinner with us, and returned to our hotel exhausted and ready for a rest.

We met Marshall that evening at the great *Jarasse* sea food restaurant near our former home in Neuilly-sur-Seine, a near suburb at the Pont de Neuilly stop of line #1. Just as we were about to go in, I got a wild hair to try to find another old favorite, the "*Le Pied dans L'Eau*" (Foot in the Water) on the nearby Ile de La Jatte, an island in the Seine River which starts at the pont and used to contain only playing fields and a few restaurants, accessible by foot only. 'Le Pied' had been a picturesque dive that featured the world's greatest Moules (Mussels). By now, however, the Ile was thoroughly developed with high-rises and streets and automobiles. The restaurant, which may have been at the same site, had been rebuilt into a slick very expensive bistro, which did not have Moules, at least not this night. We were too tired to walk back to *Jarasse* and settled for some nondescript appetizers and called it a night.

On Wednesday, we decided to do something new - a 3 mile boat ride down the St. Martin canal which ended at the old Napoleonic arsenal at the Bastille. It was fun ride, past the new Science Museum through the heart of the city. There were three 2-level locks on the way, and the last half mile was through a scary underground grotto. After lunch near the marina at the Port de L'Arsenal, we Metroed back to Neuilly to see our old neighborhood and take a walk in the adjacent Bois de Bologne. Our former house, 5 Ter, Rue du General Henrion Bertier, was as lovely as ever, although its garage appeared to have been converted, and the building itself appeared to be attached to the building behind it. Perhaps it was now a 3-4 family condo? After the Bois, we went back to the Monoprix to stock up our "water" bottles for tomorrow's trans-Atlantic flight. We agonized as to where we should have our final dinner in Paris- Jarasse or L'Entrecote?

5 TER RUE DU GENERAL HENRION BERTIER

We wanted to have a go at the wonderful Belon oysters (when we lived there, I would frequently pick up a dozen at the stand outside *Jarasse* on my way home, and soon became a skilled shucker). We decided that we could always get good sea food in the harbor across the street at home, and opted for L'Entrecote, with a prior stop for oysters at the sea food place near it. It turned out to be an expensive decision- the dozen oysters and glasses of wine cost $50- but what the hay- it was our last night in Paree!

We had a 2 p.m. Icelandic flight to Boston (via a stop in Reykjavik - which, at least from the air and in the vicinity of the airport, didn't even look like a nice place to visit) and asked the desk clerk at the hotel to arrange for a shuttle to take us to Charles de Gaulle airport. This is a new service which the clerk said was very dependable. To make sure, we asked for a 10:30 pickup, and did not panic until 11:30 - at which time we got a cab (Never thinking of using the rail line whose station was right beneath us- though it would have been hard to get the baggage down the Metro steps).

We were met at Logan by son Jeffrey, and his entourage - medium pregnant Lori; their now very voluble and adorable daughter, Emily Ann; and their huge Akita, Kobe, and whisked off to Swampscott for our final week. This happy visit at their new home included several trips to the beach (the weather was great!); a few bouts with lobsters and clams; an evening at Fenway Park, watching the Sox beat the Rangers and finally seeing the "Green Monster" wall in person; reunions with old grad school -and-since friends, the Brooks; and a lovely Sunday excursion to a local horse show and a polo match (for me, the first such since my New York days in the late 40's when we used to watch the several extant 10 goal players in Westchester county go at it on the weekends). But, the most fun was playing and talking with Miss Emily - our only girl grandchild- soon, any day now as I finished this epic on August 12, 1999 - to be joined by a sister whose name probably will be Caroline.

We were glad to get home- and were left to remember the highlights with great fondness: The Taj; the cancelled wedding; finding the bus to Amman; the camcorder loss; seeing our relatives and friends in Israel as well as in Germany, France, and Massachusetts. On arrival, we learned of a sad event. "Uncle" (actually first cousin) Harold Brodsky of Philadelphia - the family Patriarch- had died at ~ 83 from a probable after-effect of a back operation - while we were in Paris. I then became the Brodsky family Patriarch.

Chapter 3

AMERICANS IN PARIS - 1969

In the early '60s, my outfit, Aerojet-General of Azusa and Sacramento, itself a part of the General Tire and Rubber Company of Akron, Ohio, bought up a small hi-tech company called Space Electronics. This Glendale company, headed by James Fletcher – destined to later become the head of NASA, and Frank Lehan – whose connections to the spook world would later draw several of my friends towards the Langley, Virginia headquarters of the CIA, was expert in space communications and allied specialties. The idea was to merge it with my Aerojet Space Division outfit to form a company that could compete with the major aerospace systems companies, like Lockheed, Boeing, Martin-Marietta, and McDonnell/Douglas. In a grand splurge, Aerojet formed a subsidiary "Space-General", and built it a new campus in El Monte, across the street from the equally new 'Black Box' that would become Aerojet's Corporate office building. After running and winning several successful proposals for new business for the new conglomeration, I was promoted to Chief Engineer.

The Space-General Corporation simply did not take off and grow as had been anticipated at its inception in 1961. This, in spite of a corps of top flight engineers, we couldn't seem to win the 'big ones'. I suspect we tried to bite off more than we could chew. In 1968, after a series of management changes, it was decided to re-absorb it back into Aerojet-General, the mother company. About that time, I got a letter from my friend Howard, who was running the Aerojet corporate office in Paris, saying that after almost 5 years in Europe, he and his wife were ready to come home. He said he would back my petition to take his place, if I wanted to try for it. Buffeted about by uncertainty on the home front, desiring a new totally different experience, and after getting concurrence from my wife and 4 kids, I did!

The big adventure began on an Air France night flight from LA to Paris. I was flying First Class-for the first time in my life - because company policy dictated that if you flew Red Eye, you flew First Class. Shortly after reaching cruise altitude, La Hotesse presented me with the menu. I quickly saw that I would have no trouble in reading French despite the fact that my three years of language courses in high school were not big on food items. However, I did see that I would now face the first big decision on my new assignment. Three equally wondrous entrees were carefully described on the menu, and I pondered mightily while waiting for the stylishly dressed young lady to ask my choice. She never did. As the night went on, each entrée was served deliciously and impeccably in the order listed. Thus, I got my first true insight into l'essence Francaise. This just added to the excitement, trepidation and anticipation of what lay in store for me.

It was mid-May 1969. I was on my way towards a one month indoctrination visit to learn the ropes of my new job. I was in my eleventh year of employment at Aerojet-General/Azusa and its subsidiary, Space-General / El Monte. Recently, massive reorganizations had begun as my newly defunct outfit was being absorbed back into the parent company. With my new assignment came a transfer into the Aerojet Corporate staff. A few months earlier, seeing that the end was near, I had applied for, and won, the plush assignment of managing Aerojet's European Office located at 164 Avenue de Neuilly in *Neuilly-sur-Seine*, an integrated township of Paris, on the northern edge of the Bois de Boulogne. The Avenue was the western extension of the Champs d'Elysees, and is now called the Ave. Charles de Gaulle. The office, and our prospective house, were both located near the Pont de Neuilly, at the Ave. de Madrid terminus of the Metro#1 line. The plan was for me to get acquainted with my new surroundings, and make the necessary arrangements for housing and schooling for my wife and four children. I would return to California in about a month, after school was out, and bring the family back to France for the duration of our tour. We had agreed that we would be willing to stay at least three years.

After my selection, my new boss, Bill Gore, the corporate International VP, told me that I had won the hotly contested Paris derby because of several factors: I was solidly backed by the four plus year job incumbent, my old friend Howard Robbins; other assets they considered were that I was even tempered, not rash; easy to talk to if not outright voluble; and a good manager who could not be bullied. They also felt that I had a certain amount of sophistication to go with my fearless smattering of French. Also, I would be addressed as Le Docteur Brodsky or Herr Doktor Brodsky - and they believed that Europeans were more impressed by titles than the average American. Unsaid, however, was the factor that I was a staunch and active Democrat in a management that was led by Democrats.

More specific, though, was the fact that I was intimately involved in rocket vehicle development and had participated in the development of an unique automated medicine device which we had just developed. Management felt that the latter might be a big seller in Western Europe, and that I could build on the start that Robbins had made in the rocket technology area. However these attributes notwithstanding, I've always believed that an additional unstated factor in selecting me was that they were about to reorganize me out of my Chief Engineer's job, since there already was an incumbent in Azusa. I accepted the job readily, after getting the wholehearted endorsement of my family. The challenge was impressive: I had never been to Europe or dealt with people on an international level. I was both scared of and eager for a real change in life style.

The Paris office, as I was about to take it over, consisted of the Director, an office manager (in this case, one Gudrun Rosner, now LaDoire) who was not only the real brains of the gang but also was fluent in English, French, Spanish and her native German, a consultant - in this case the defrocked former Director, and a large highly-detailed three dimensional map of Paris glued to a wall. This small enclave had been operating gloriously in the black for several years, being credited with a few million dollars per year in pure profit from the royalties obtained from NATO's use of an Aerojet patent and technical support covering the manufacture of the rocket motors which powered the Hawk surface-to-air missile; then the bulwark of the West's NATO defense system.

In fact, these royalties were the prime reason that Aerojet maintained a European base, which had been established shortly after rocket motor production in Europe had begun. The other income from the technical support of French and ESRO (European Space Research Organization) experimental rocket programs, which Robbins had promoted and was leaving for me to continue, paid for our daily baguettes and office expenses. Although other ventures were in the offing, none appeared capable of approaching the NATO financial harvest anticipated from future Hawk missile royalties. The Hawk rocket motors were being manufactured under our license by the French (by the Ministry de Poudres, Toulouse), by the Germans (at Waldkraiburg, east of Munich), and by the Italians (at Colleferro, near Rome). When I arrived, the initially contracted production run was almost over and negotiations for follow-on production were already under way.

My instructions from the International VP were few and, so I thought, relatively straightforward: Keep Aerojet's flag waving in Europe by becoming a member of the international community in Paris; take good care of all visiting firemen, be they Aerojetters, customers, or potential customers; manage the English-to-French translation of the operation and maintenance documents of the satellite communication station we were building in Morocco; but do not ask questions about and forward, without opening, monthly statements concerning a Moroccan bank account maintained at our office's bank; support the NATO program as first priority, especially by trying to move the negotiations along; support the French and ESRO rocket programs as second priority; visit and placate M. Samuel at Compagnie Sedam once a month and, if supplied from the US, show him new pages of a revised Air Cushioned Vehicle design royalty agreement between Aerojet and Sedam; try to sell our automated syphilis test machine and required serum to all Western nations; assist the French high tech development company, Bertin & Cie, on mutually undertaken proposals; and – beatifically - enjoy the experience, remembering that money was no object.

Only the 'Bank' advice puzzled me. Much later, I learned that the envelope contained 'baksheesh', a helpful monetary addition to the Moroccan government official responsible for getting power and water to the remote telecommunications construction site, outside of Rabat. There, we were building a communications satellite ground station destined to free all of North Africa from the very high tariff the French telephone company that 'owned' the underwater cable between Morocco and France charged for the service. Now, long distance calls from all of North Africa were affordable to 'plain' folks.

The next morning, Howard and Gudrun met me at Orly, whence my training began. Happily, the semi-rigorous agenda allowed for sight seeing in Paris and included attending the famous Paris Air Show at Le Bourget, where Lindy had landed many years ago. Here, I was impressed by the amount of commerce going on in the various chalets where the great aerospace companies of the world presided over vast quantities of free food and drink and, I suspect, women.

During my month introductory visit, I made arrangements to buy the Robbins' *Peugeot 404* (quatre cent quatre) with its Florida license plates, and to take over the company-paid lease of their house on Cinq Ter Rue du General Henrion Bertier; learned to pronounce Neuilly almost accurately, but struggled mightily and, to this day to no avail, to correctly pronounce Roule, as in Ave de - and Hotel de- where I stayed during this initial visit. The damned silent "e" at the end somehow gets pronounced in a way that only Parisians can do. For example, I could always "hear" Gudrun's "e"s, even though she was a Bavarian by birth, but clearly now a Parisian.

I quickly learned my way around the city, aided no end by the graphic map which covered one wall of the office foyer. It turned out that for the most part, our main business could be accomplished by walking to the nearby NATO and ESRO headquarters. I soon learned the Metro system almost by heart. By happenstance, an ego-boosting linguistic triumph occurred early in the game. I had descended into the Pont de Neuilly metro station on my way to the Louvre and almost ran over a Chinese kid. He was obviously lost, and even had his Metro map upside down. With my newly gained confidence, I went up to him and said, "Puis je vous aidez, Monsieur?" He stammered back, "I don't speak French. Do you know English?" "Certainement, Monsieur", I replied. "Where do you wish to go?" We then discussed his train options until he knew what he had to do. As we parted, he thanked me profusely and told me how well I spoke English. "Merci millefois, Monseiur. C'etait mon plaisir", I signed off without batting an eyelash or a smile.

During the month visit, Howard took me on the business "rounds". I met the NATO major domos in Paris, just before NATO Headquarters moved to Brussels. I gathered that the follow-on contract negotiations were going slowly - not so much because Aerojet had asked for a few royalty dollars more per rocket motor - but because the countries involved could not get together. They were arguing among themselves about schedules and urgency, numbers, deployment sites and technical improvements. It did not occur to me then that when the production lines stopped, so did the royalties and, consequently, the Office black ink record. But I did get a kick out of talking with and being treated deferentially by the NATO General Officers. I was not that far away from being of Seaman First Class rank in the US Navy. In my first encounter with them, I noted that the language of NATO was English, so my technical French was not yet put to the test.

We next visited the licensed rocket motor production sites. The most interesting of these was the German installation, whose factory layout had been designed by the Aerojet Solid Rocket plant in Sacramento. They had also supplied the huge batch mixers where the very unstable propellant was prepared for pouring into the motor casings. We drove there in a rental car that we had picked up at the Munich airport. Waldkraiburg is a sylvan town in the midst of a large forest, through which meanders a narrow gauge railroad. The Inn River is nearby, as is the Austrian border, and Innsbruck. We stayed at a German motel (motels were new in Germany) and paid about $2 US each for a room. We noted that an additional motel building was in the first stages of construction. A year later, when I made the visit to commemorate the end of the initial rocket motor production contract, the motel proprietor apologized profusely for charging me $2.50 per night. He blamed it on the higher than expected cost of building the expansion. I told him my company could probably afford that added burden.

The completely camouflaged rocket motor fabrication plant itself was right out of James Bond! Entry was gained by a passage that closely paralleled the hidden ingress tunnel of the narrow gauge railway siding. The entire huge plant was covered by six feet of dirt on which grass and trees were growing. We were told that the original plant was the biggest producer of gun powder in Germany during World War II, and the Allies never knew it existed! The sod over the roof also served the double duty of containing the effects of a possible batch mixer explosion, a not unusual occurrence at such plants. The inside of the plant was pristine, and never had a problem during my watch. Most of the officials we dealt with spoke English fluently, so I was thwarted, again, in trying out my prowess in German, learned in childhood from my German nurse and in graduate school (along with refreshing my French) in order to pass my Doctorate language requirements.

Such was not true in Colleferro. Only one person there at the plant spoke English, and naturally he became our guide and interpreter. I didn't dare try out my newly learned Italian, especially since when earlier I had tried ordering at restaurants the prior evening and at breakfast, the waiters inevitably pleaded "Please speak English!" Years later, I returned to Colleferro on an adjunct inspection trip from an International Astronautics Federation meeting taking place in Rome. Now, everyone spoke English and the greatly enlarged complex had become the leading center for Italian rocket research.

Another introductory trip we took was to the ESRO (now, ESA - European Space Agency) research and development labs in Noordwijk, Holland. This lovely North Sea beach city is about 40 miles southwest of Amsterdam. We stayed in an early version of a B&B – an old white Victorian former mansion - right at the beach. Robbins had been working with the ESRO sounding rocket group who were adapting the Aerojet scientific instrument space-experiment pointing control system, which Howard had developed, to the British "Skylark" sounding rocket vehicle. The Skylark was scheduled to carry scientific instruments into space from a launch in Woomera, Australia. The group's supervisor was a Dutchman, Koos Leertouwer. In his group were two Englishmen, a Spaniard, and several Frenchmen, Germans, Dutchmen and Italians. As we shmoozed with him, his multi-lingual troops would knock on his door and speak with him, each in their native language. He replied in kind without losing a beat. Oh, how I envied him! I was still struggling to speak English precisely and slowly enough so that foreigners could understand my native Philadelphia tongue, let alone me trying to speak theirs.

The final first-round trip was to Bretigny-sur-Seine where CNES, the French counterpart of NASA, maintained its sounding rocket base. We drove the 404 about 30 miles south of Paris, passing the then small town of Evry. Today, Evry is heavily developed with modern buildings, and is a major ESA center which controls the European launch vehicle, Ariane, and the ESA launch base near Devil's Island in French Guiana in South America. Entering Bretigny, we drove through the exquisitely drab, but highly picturesque, narrow-streeted sidewalkless medieval town, down to the ramshackle buildings that abutted what was undeniably a World War I aerodrome.

Here, Jean-Max de La Mar held court with his group devoted to carrying French-developed scientific instruments to a 5 minute or more ride in near space. Robbins was working with them adapting three of his space instrument - pointing control systems, the same system that the Noordwyjk bunch were adapting for the *Skylark*, into their *Veronique* sounding rocket. This remarkable vehicle did not require a launch tower to make sure it stayed on course as it accelerated off of the launch pad. Since the rocket's speed was too low to make them effective at the beginning of launch, the vehicle's four tail fins could not provide proper guidance at low speed. In other systems, like Aerojet's famous *Aerobee* sounders, this is overcome by the use of a launch tower. Ingeniously, the French connected wires, from the aft tip of each of the fins, which unreeled as the rocket rose. The tension in the equal length unreeling wires kept the vehicle going straight up! When, after a couple hundred of feet unreeled, *Veronique* was going fast enough to allow its tail fins to provide guidance, the wires disconnected and fell back to earth. Our sounding rockets required a massive 150 foot tower for launch, as well as a separate powerful first stage booster rocket motor which accelerated it to the same speed, in its 150 foot constrained run up the tower, as the *Veronique* attained at 200-plus feet when its wires dropped away. Although the French system seemed a little like the Toonerville Trolley, it did save the cost of a tower and the cost and handling of a separate boost motor. Vive La France!

Howard told me a story of earlier watching the first *Veronique* flight which carried his control system as it was launched in Algeria. This trip occurred before the "troubles" arose between the French and the Algerians, who sought to reclaim their country. CNES then used a launch base at Hamaguir, a stark desert test base area about 400 miles south-southwest of Algiers at the foothills of the Atlas mountain range. Howard, Jean Max, and another CNES rocketeer (Jean-Pierre Morin, who later became the first station head of the now huge ESA launch base in Guiana) landed in Algiers and were picked up by a driver from the launch base. They were shocked to see that their automotive vehicle was a *Deux Chevaux*, a very basic bottom-of-the-line Citroen sedan (its nick-name "Two Horses" adequately describes its engine's ability). This wonderful vehicle, then selling brand new for about $600 American, had seats of cloth stretched over metal bars- much like a cot. Obviously, they were not built for comfort, but to go 400 miles through a stifling desert was the stuff heroes are made of!

Howard could not, for the life of him, see how the driver knew where he was going since whatever road they were supposed to be on was long ago covered with drifting sand. When asked, the driver said he navigated by looking for strategically placed reflectors, nailed to the tops of sticks, which were not covered by sand. During preparation for the launch, another unusual incident occurred. Howard and his bunch were proceeding to the launch pad, when another *Deux Chevaux*, returning from the pad, approached them. What ensued, in that vast no-man's land of a featureless desert, was the old narrow sidewalk game of trying to pass an approaching pedestrian. Both cars bobbed, feinted, and weaved, but inevitably hit head on. No one was seriously hurt, but they were stranded in the desert for a couple of hours, since these were the days before cell phones. After the ride and the crash, Howard reported the ensuing launch was anti-climactic.

The introductory phase being completed, I returned home to California to make my report to the family and get ready for our migration. As I flew back, I mused about my feelings about my first contact with a new and somewhat strange world. All during the month, I had had an almost Alice-in-Wonderland aura about seeing so many strange sights and talking to so many different types of people. In retrospect, I decided that I liked the insouciance of the French, despite the Parisians disdain of poorly spoken French and foreign mode of dress. I greatly appreciated the fact that Europe appeared to be very civilized and the people very tolerant. I thought that I was going to relish the experience ahead of me, and hoped my family would feel likewise. Now, the adventure would soon begin for all of us.

Dr. R. F. Brodsky

Manager European Operations
Aerojet-General Corporation

164 Ave. de Neuilly
92 Neuilly s. Seine

624. 32-50

Chapter 4

THE ROAD TO MAROC - 1969

A surprising one-in-a-million even took place on the ferry boat going back from *Tangiers*, Morocco to Algeciras, Spain where our car was parked. About halfway across the Sea, amid all the chatter in French, we heard a loud English-speaking voice say, "My God, it's the Brodsky's!" The voice belonged to a good friend who taught at Pomona College in Claremont, where we normally lived. It turned out he was on a sabbatical at the University of Rabat. What a small world!

But first let's review the circumstances of our being on the ferry: Dan Kimbell, the President of Aerojet-General, was a good personal friend of the late King Hassan of Morocco. Their friendship started when Dan had earlier established a General Tire plant in the kingdom. They were very comfortable and trustful with each other in business dealings. So, when Morocco wanted to build a satellite communications ground station to handle all telephone traffic from North Africa, they sole-sourced the job to Aerojet / Space General. But, we still had to make a proposal to make it official. I was responsible for the writing of the Business Management volume of this 1968 tome. It was our first job of developing such a ground station.

The station would free the North African continent from the iron grip of the French national telephone company. They were handling all the telephone and wire traffic, via a cable laid on the bottom of the Mediterranean Sea, and had been charging users an arm and a leg for the privilege.

Estimates were that the projected satellite communications charges, even after writing off the projected 10 million dollar cost of the ground station, would be about 20% of what they had been paying. The new low cost of communication would make phones affordable to a much larger segment of the North African population. It was clearly a win-win proposition.

After I took over managing the Aerojet office in Paris in 1969, I inherited the responsibility of translating the station's operating documents from Space General-generated English into French. I quickly got bogged down trying to do it myself, having particular trouble finding the right French words for the technical components. After a while, I decided to hire a French firm to do the translation, and they appeared to be doing a good job, which I closely monitored. After they had produced a couple hundred pages, I thought I'd better take them down to Rabat. There, I would check their comprehension with the French engineers whom the Moroccan phone company had hired both to run the station as well as to train native Moroccan engineers, who would eventually take over the complete operation.

We, my wife, our 4 year old son, and I, drove to Algeciras, Spain, took the ferry to Tangiers, and the train to Rabat - a very picturesque trip. Along the stark desert route, we saw several caravans – each consisting of 20 or more camels all in a row and managed by at least 10 'camel jockeys'. Quite a sight – right from the bible! We were met at the train station by Space-General employee, Arabic-speaking Dave Darakjy, who was in charge of station construction. He checked us into the hotel, showed us around the city, and arranged for shipping, for free, a newly purchased Moroccan rug back to California via an Army friend of his who was returning home. I had been in the vicinity of

Rabat, at its harbor, Port Lyautey, for a short stay during WWII. However, on my sole liberty venture into town there, I immediately and violently contracted ptomaine right after my first dinner ashore and had to be dragged back to the ship's sick bay; so I had no previous in-depth recollection of the city.

He took us out to the site, about 20 miles NW of Rabat, the next morning, stopping first a makeshift outdoor market, a souk (pronounced 'shuke') which was located a few hundred yards from the site. The souk was a sight to behold! It was a throwback to biblical times. Twice a week, the local Bedouin population would ride in on their donkeys, some coming great distances, to shop at the informal market. The Bedouins were hand-some, tall people with blue eyes. They "parked" their donkeys in the most raucous, noisy, smelly, lascivious parking lot you've ever seen or sniffed. Two attendants, armed with long boards, tried half-heartedly to maintain the peace by swatting the males as they attempted to mount the females. Our son couldn't figure out what was going on.

The souk had everything a Bedouin could need. There were open fires where you could buy grilled sandwiches, barber shops, pita bakeries, clothes stores, produce and meat stores, wine sellers, etc. The butcher 'shop' featured camel's heads, apparently a delicacy. I suspect that their life style had not changed for generations. Dave told us that the people who frequented the souk had absolutely no idea what the crazy people in the government were building, and dismissed the construction as nonsense. We took many pictures using our son as the focus. The Bedouins believed that if you took their pictures, you were robbing their souls.

When we got there, the people at the site were all grousing because the Minister of Telephony had not yet provided power or tap water from the city, as promised. They had to use generators which were balky and get water delivered by a truck. This, in spite of the expected effect of what I was sure was a 'baksheesh' envelop which I processed to a Moroccan Ministry through my Paris office once a month, without knowing its contents.

The huge 90 foot diameter antenna was being assembled by our subcontractor, Rohr Aircraft of San Diego, using prefabricated parts shipped from the US. Moroccan building contractors had constructed the fixed installations. I conducted my business and soon found that the first contingent of French engineers hired to run the station were happy with the translated operations manual portion that I reviewed with them. I could therefore give a favorable progress report to the people back home, while urging more pressure on the defaulting, but otherwise prosperous, Communications Minister to meet his commitments. Shortly thereafter both power and water suddenly appeared at the site, but I could swear the monthly envelope was heavier.

That evening, Dave escorted us through the Casbah. My wife spotted a tschotke that she liked for which the vendor wanted $10. Dave stepped in and said, "Let me do the negotiating". The conversation in Arabic was heated and interminable. Finally Dave said, "Let's get out of here". Sure enough, as we left the shop the poor merchant came racing after us, agreeing to a $2 sale. Dave was merciless at bargaining- an ability that completely escapes me. He looked on it as a sport. We then ate at a fine restaurant which featured soft couches on which you draped yourself, while watching a wonderful belly dancer, and eating the meat and chicken couscous entrée by scooping it out of a bowl using your first two fingers. It was delicious.

The station turned out to be a smashing success, and has helped to bring Morocco, Algeria, Libya, Tunisia, and Egypt, all connected by hard line, in better tune with the outside world. The inauguration ceremony, attended by an impressive number of high placed Moroccan and US officials, including the King, was marred only by the fact that the French engineers were still in charge. This situation was corrected a few years later, and the King's five million dollar investment in the Aerojet part of the project has been repaid many times.

Chapter 5

EGYPT - 1989

One of the most impressive and exciting trips we ever took resulted from our first 'visiting professor' stay (at the Technion in Haifa) in Israel. It came at the time of the Hannukah break in school (in December very near Xmas, this year), and coincided with visits from both the Newbrough's of Iowa and the Gazin's of Hermosa Beach, who were our traveling companions after we had guided them on the official 'Brodsky Tour' of Israel. We joined a Technion Group on a week-long visit to Egypt, at a time when political relations between the two countries were exemplary. We had an Israeli guide with us – a very knowledgeable man – indeed one who knew more about Egyptian history than the Cairo University-trained professional guides that we, as a tourist group, were required to hire at each major site. Fortunately, Pat made notes of the trip, and we developed a notated trip 'book' with many pictures – two of which will be seen below.

We started the adventure at the Ben Gurion airport, which is located in between Jerusalem and Tel Aviv, around 10ish in the evening. The Cairo airport waiting area, where we found ourselves after debarkation, was a mass of humanity covering a full city block. Don made a makeshift sign attached to a stick he found and paraded around. It said, "*Brodsky*". Finally we were gathered up by a tour director and bused, seemingly a long way, through Cairo to our suburb hotel destination, the SIAG Pyramids Hotel in Giza. We immediately had dinner. When we finally got to bed, the time was almost 2 a.m., and we were directed to have our bags in the hallway at 6 a.m. – ready to go touring.

After a short sleep, we awakened and Pat opened up the window curtains, and gasped! Right in front of us, within 300 yards, were the Pyramids and the Sphinx in all their early sunrise glory. We were overwhelmed by the sheer glory of the scene – the 3 huge pyramids and the Sphinx – bathed in the early morning sunlight. We boarded a bus after breakfast and were taken to the Pyramids and Sphinx, and thence to Saqqara, where there was a smaller pyramid and hundreds of tombs and monuments. We rode through country that was a throwback to B.C.E times - camels and donkey-pulled carts – the whole 9 yards. Pat bought a wall hanging at a rug factory stop and lugged it around for the rest of the trip. We stopped for an outdoor lunch on the way to Memphis. Featured there is a huge limestone statue of Ramses II. Then, back to Cairo to get a bus-eye view of the city. Notable was the huge garbage repository area, in which many people lived. Apparently they gather and sold 'valuables' that came with the refuse. Also noteworthy was he remains of the old (way B.C.E.) synagogue. On our way back to Haifa at the end of the week, we would have a detailed city tour, described later.

GIZA- VIEW FROM HOTEL

We took the over night train from Cairo to Luxor. We had a comfortable compartment, ate dinner (I, a foreign guest - did the blessing at the lighting of that night's Hanukah candle – and arrived at 8:30 the next morning. Thoughtfully, they played Hebrew music in our dining area, mixed with Christmas music. We stayed at the fine ISIS Hotel Luxor, arriving on Christmas Eve day. The two outstanding tourist sites on the east side of the river are Luxor's two ancient temples, *Luxor* and *Karnak*. From 2100 to 750 B.C.E., Egyptian power and glory centered in these Temples, which were amazingly well preserved and noble in appearance. *Luxor* presented a huge roomful of magnificent, 6 foot diameter columns which supported the roof of the main temple building. *Karnak* was more spread-out, city-like. Its entry-way was guarded by a coterie of very large statues of lions- one next to the other – at least 30 of them. We attended a spectacular sound and light ('Son et Lumiere') show amidst the huge structures – statues and 10 foot diameter columns. Again we were amazed at how well these structures had survived the passage of significant time.

After lunch, we were ferried over the Nile to the Western side into the Valley of the - Kings, and then – of the Queens. At the entry into the valley was the town of Haru, which features a very large auditorium-like building, whose entry way was guarded by two 30 feet tall statues. The valleys were real eye-openers. There to be inspected were the burial sites of ancient royalty, and their coteries and prize possessions – all preserved as if they were sealed yesterday. They were built into hollowed-out hills, and led into by a narrow tunnel. The brightly colored tunnel wall paintings were not in the least faded. Perhaps the reason for this is that the Valleys were fairly recent discoveries and more 'new' crypts are being discovered every so often. In the main burial room, the crypt was in the center, with other graves in monuments strewn around along with the treasures. It was breathtaking - the art work fantastic! We returned exhausted, to be regaled with a Christmas Eve feast to end a long exciting day, in wonderment of the splendor that must have been 4000-5000 BC Egypt.

Christmas day, we left by bus to Aswan, a 5 hour drive away. Enroute, we stopped ~midway at the Fortress-like *Temple of Edfu*. It is reputed to be the best preserved of the temples. We also stopped at the *Hathor Temple* a bit further down the road. Neither of these - while interesting – matched the magnificence of *Luxor* and *Karnac*. We were taken directly to the airport that serves Aswan and flown south, by EgyptAir, to Abu Simbel, at the far end of Lake Nasser (formed by the great Aswan dam). Before they filled the lake, the government moved the great statuary that we were going to see to a newly erected facility on high ground. This was a major work of engineering. The problem was moving the main feature, the Ramses II statuary – carved out of a rock hill side, and recreating the original with fidelity. This was done most successfully.

ABU SIMBEL

When we came to the four sitting-side-by-side 40-50 foot high re-located statues, we found ourselves standing with our mouths agape! How did they do it? Two of the sitting figures were badly deteriorated – not caused by the move. Still, the scene is majestic and awesome. The statuary guarded the entrance to the museum they had created in the cleared-out inside of the hill utilizing other pieces from the now underwater site. Again, these ancient artifacts were well preserved. We then flew back to Aswan for late festive dinner at the Amon Village Hotel and sleep. Our group also appropriately celebrated the 4th night of Hanukah. What a full delightful Christmas Day!!

Amon Village itself proved to be a shopper and sightseers delight ("We Wright Your Name In Hirogliphic"). After we spent some time looking around the grounds after breakfast, the bus picked us up for an all day tour. Aswan is a bustling city, with a somewhat lurid history. When they decided to dam up the river to have better control of the all-important fertilizing silt that kept the Nile banks alive, they hired the Russians as overseeing consultants. Apparently, after a long hard effort, they didn't succeed in finding a good solution to include locks - for fish to swim through; and to control the all-important silt. Americans took over and eventually succeeded, so by the time we arrived all was well and quite settled. There was a lot to see.

An interesting stop was at the site of an abandoned, in construction, Obelisk. It was in the process of being carved out of rock in a horizontal position. The one we saw was about 70 feet long and at least 10 feet at the base, in a Washington Monument configuration. Three sides were finished, and somehow the underside was cut through the rock, and the column then 'rolled' out of the hole for 4th side finishing and later transportation to its destination. We inspected the dam and saw the vast Lake Nasser that the dam had created and over which we had flown to Abu Simbel. The river was very wide at the bottom of the dam. We would later have a sail on it. Also in the vicinity was a lovely white marble lotus-shaped monument dedicated to the Russian effort.

On the western bank above the dam, in a harbor cove, awaited a fleet of Feluccas – Egyptian wooden sailboats about 20 feet or more long and ~6 feet in beam. They carried a single large triangular sail mounted on a long pole that attached to the top of the mast. So, part of the sail acted as a jib, and the rest – aft of the mast – as the mainsail. They carried 6 people comfortably. I was itching to take control, and was permitted to do so. It was a warm day with a good breeze. We sailed by two large islands, one - Elephantine Island, had what appeared to be a government building on it; the other, Kitcheners Island, was a botanical garden. We were left off on the west bank, where a further adventure awaited us.

We landed amidst a coterie of camels, each saddled up with an accompanying camel jockey. The offer was a mile ride up a fairly steep slope to the Monastery of San Simeon. The Gazins opted out; the Newbroughs decided on a two-passenger camel, and Pat and I on single camels. About 20 camels were in our caravan, including – right in back of us – Abe Goldberg of Chicago (you've got to bear with me for this aside story). Pat described the process of getting ready for the long march: "It's when the camel stands up (from its kneeling position when you mount) that you begin to know you're in trouble. As his rear legs straighten, you fall forward – you swear you're going to fall off and land on your nose; then all of a sudden you're sitting way up there in the air". I can't imagine what this two-step camel mount was like for the Newbroughs. All in line, our caravan started up the steep pathway through the desert.

The excitement started about half way up after we had seen, to the left of us about another mile away, the tomb of the Aga Khan, when I heard Abe, with a big smile of his face, say to his camel, "Oy!, Oy! I knew what that meant. Abe's jockey had previously told him that the camels, who he said were trained by Bedouins in Israel and only understood Hebrew, would move forward on the "Oy!" command and would stop at "Shalom!" So Abe happily pulled out from the caravan line and went traipsing over the desert at a trot. Then I heard him say "Oy!, Oy!Oy!" and he was off on a gallop - jockey left in his wake. Suddenly he saw that he was approaching a treacherous deep cliff. At the very last moment, he remembered to shout "Shalom", and his camel landed on all four feet right at the edge of the cliff. Abe leaned back in his saddle, wiped off his sweaty brow, and breathed a sigh of relief, and said: "Oy!" **(you see what I mean?).**

We inspected the monastery, with its above ground crypts that held the remains of past monks and commanded a beautiful view of the desert. We repeated the tricky dismount maneuver back in the camel parking lot. It was a wonderful, unique (how many people you know have ridden on a camel?) experience. We flew back to Cairo that night, ready for a full day tour of Cairo the next morning.

The major visiting sites in the capital city were the magnificent *Mohammed Aly Mosque* ("The Citadel"), the equally ornate *El Sultan Hassan* and the *Al Rifai* Mosques (the latter had a beautiful clock tower with a 'Big Ben' type French clock on one side), the oldest synagogue in Cairo, *Ben Ezra*, and the place where we spent most of the time – The Egyptian State Museum. Here, the treasures of ancient Egypt were displayed, including the King Tut exhibit that tours the world's museums. There were multitudes of breathtakingly beautiful artifacts. Clearly this place was a national treasure.

The trip ended with a final party/dinner sendoff at our hotel, and a day long bus trip from Cairo back to Haifa. We were ferried over the Suez Canal, and drove through stark desert to Rafah, the Egyptian town abutting the south end of the Gaza Strip. We drove up the Gaza Strip on the Israeli side of the fence, and made it 'home' uneventfully after one of the two best trips of our lives. About 10 days later, the February 5, 1990 edition of the English language '*Jerusalem*

POST' screamed its headline, "10 Slain as terrorists hit Israeli Tour in Egypt". The article said, "Masked terrorists, firing semi-automatic weapons and hurling hand grenades, killed at least 10 passengers, eight of them Israelis, on an Egyptian tour bus, 50-60 kms. east of Cairo near the town of Ismailiya at 4:30 yesterday afternoon." On reading this, we leaned back, wiped our brows, and said "OY"!

Chapter 6

THE ORIENTAL STRUT[2]- 1995

(Hong Kong, Tokyo/Japan, & China)

By the spring of 1995, we had well over a 100,000 American Airlines 'Frequent Flyer' miles saved up. Most of these had accrued as a result of our return to Israel to teach at the TECHNION in Haifa for the spring semester in 1994. Wanting our kids to share in the experience, we had provided all four with round-trip airline tickets so that they might visit while we were there. Where we could, we took mileage credit as the purchasers of the tickets. We had always wanted to visit the Orient, and now the time was right. Previously, in the early 50's when I went to Eniwetok for an A-bomb test, I had been reasonably close to the main land; but had no chance to go sightseeing. We now had the transportation and financial means as well as a built-in family guide in Hong Kong, where son David's in-laws lived. We also had the time- since my USC class's final exam was early in May and I had no other commitments until mid-June. We organized the trip!

In addition to Hong Kong, We also wanted to see a bit of Japan and China. We planned for a few days in Tokyo with a side trip to the shrine city of Nikko, about 100 miles north of Tokyo My USC class TV operator (my courses had both a live audience and a national TV hook-up) was a Japan buff, and told us what we should

2 From Louis Armstrong's "Oriental Strut"

do in Japan and that we should stay at a Ryokan - a Japanese business- man's type Mom and Pop inn in the Ueno Park section. Foreigners generally do not stay in such a hotel, but she wanted us to get a more intimate view of Japanese life.

In China, we of course wanted to see the Great Wall and the Forbidden City in Beijing (as well as have a reunion with a Chinese aerospace engineer whom I had invited to spend two years as a visiting scientist in my Department at Iowa State University in the 70's). We also wanted to see the famed terra cotta army in Xi'an, and were shilled by friends to add a boat trip down the river Li out of Guilin, to see the unique saw-toothed mountains.

We had a total of over a week in Hong Kong, and left our itinerary there up to our son's Mother-in-Law. We did, however, want to stay on both Hong Kong Island and Kowloon. We started on the island, staying near the night club district at a time when the US fleet was in. We spent some time talking to Shore Patrol tars, normally not my friends, swapping stories about how things were in the States as opposed to the joys of shore leave in oriental ports of call. This provided an easy transition into a new world. The trip was fabulous! Upon our return - fired up by enthusiasm - I set down the following trip documentation in May 1995:

"HEREIN, A KALEIDOSCOPIC ACCOUNT OF OUR TRIP TO THE MYSTERIOUS EAST

We're back!! - back from the rigors of fighting the huddling masses, the fleets of bicycles (we saw many "Pick-Up" truck varieties carrying four seated passengers as well as "conventional" 2-passenger taxi-cab bikes!) in their special bike lanes adjoining the regular streets, the incredibly smelly Chinese squat-style toilets with no toilet paper, and - believe it or not - had our fill of the Jewish national dish – Chinese food; all by far magnificently counterbalanced by wondrous sights and gentle people. We've promised so many of our friends a true account of our May 6-24 jaunt to Hong Kong, Tokyo/Nikko, and China (Guilin, Beijing, Xi'an) that we decided this single opus would be most expedient as an attachment to our individual letters. This does <u>not</u> excuse <u>any</u> of you from being relieved of watching 3 hours of interminable camcorder tape coupled with detailed perusal of Pat's official illustrated trip journal on your next visit to our hallowed halls - so here goes !

Our first stop (with 2 subsequent revisits later on) was Hong Kong (which as everyone knows consists of Hong Kong Island, and Kowloon across Victoria Harbour and the continuing mainland New Territories, all scheduled to become part of mainland China in 1997, which event is being viewed optimistically by those remaining). This complex is a bustling, 7 million strong outpost of beautiful modern high rise buildings, an excellent subway/bus/ tramway/ferry local transportation system, all types of ethnic food, general prices comparable to US standards, with wonderful bargains and 'Tchotzkes' available in anything the mind can conceive of at all kinds of stores/ shops /outdoor markets. English and Mandarin are the official languages, but 95% of the population is Chinese, making for small problems (e.g., our taxi took us to two wrong YMCA hotels before finding the right "Y"!). During the entire trip, we made three separate HK forays (once on the Island, and twice in Kowloon at the 'fabulous' (i.e. modest expense) Salisbury Road YMCA which is hard-by the equally-fabled Peninsula Hotel (yes, we had high tea there); the gorgeous Cultural Center; the fabled "Star

Ferry"; and the also noted Regent Hotel, where we had the mandatory sunset cocktails (very expensive) in the company of our in-laws (son David's bride's parents- her mother, Mary Lee was a wonderful and faithful guide- who knows all the right places, having lived there for over 5 years). Some of the highlights of our wanderings were a harbor ride on a sampan- type boat (lots of activities, especially in land reclamation); a bus trip to Aberdeen via the Repulse Bay beach resort to eat at one of the great floating restaurants reached by sampan; a bus trip to Stanley Market; trips to the Kowloon Flower and Bird markets; and thence to the Prince Edward subway stop to inspect the street of outdoor markets; an open upper deck, tram (electric trolley) ride of the Hong Kong island side waterfront area with its great buildings and subsequent "walk" on the very long escalator which goes up to the mountainside condo community above the harbor; and a cable car ride to the peak, on an overcast day where, alas, we could barely see the harbor. Finally, although we were just too tired to take advantage, we noted the down-the-street appearance of a genuine New Orleans Jazz band. In summary - an exciting city where things are happening; with an excellent newspaper - the South China Post (with the same damn undecipherable Brit cross word puzzles as in the Jerusalem Post!) and a TV menu that includes CNN, Star TV, Prime Sports, BBC, etc. And, if you need a knock-off watch of any brand, where else?

HONG KONG

On to Tokyo for 3 full days, where the new airport (Narita) is a one hour train ride at 20 bucks per person from town, and the prices were about 30 - 40% higher than in the US, unless you are very careful (we were!). It is a huge (~13 million) sprawling city with a wonderful and easy to use subway/light rail transportation system which is usually very crowded- but talks to you in both Japanese and English. We did stay at the Japanese version of a B&B (a Mom and Pop hotel with maybe 20 rooms- most Japanese style) called a Ryokan. For a few bucks more, we got a western style (i.e., a bed rather than a futon) room with a western style bathroom. One must remove one's shoes before entering and wear house-supplied slippers. You also get kimonos, and it is perfectly proper to wear them when you join your hosts (who speak some English) for choice of Japanese or western style breakfast.

Tokyo is a large flat big area city, starting at Tokyo Bay and heading inland toward Mt Fuji (which we never really saw due to continued overcast). It has two main clusters of high rise buildings - the touristy Ginza section (which was disappointing, but maybe because we did not see it at night) and Shimbuku section- which is the city government and financial district. City Hall is a beautiful 50 story twin tower building with a panoramic (and free, as compared to the considerably lower poor man's Eiffel Tower-like "Tokyo Tower" of tourist fame) view of the whole city and Mt Fuji - on a clear day. The only trouble we had occurred in restaurants, where the menus are generally not in English (except in the Roppongi section- where the swingers and Caucs hang out). You make your selections by looking at pictures or "models" of the menu, but often you do not know what you are getting- but it's usually very good. We found a wonderful outdoor noodle (hot broth with noodles and lots of "fixin's") bar near our Ryokan, as well as a great sushi bar in Roppongi.

We took the morning "Citirama" bus tour, narrated in good English. We started at the posh Palace Hotel (across the street from the Emperor's palace grounds) and noted the elegantly dressed businessmen, chauffeur-driven up to the door, in their Rolls Royce-equivalent "Presidential" models (Toyota?), reminding us of the several gray Rolls taxis- and two golden ones-which take Regent's guests to the HK airport at slightly more cost than the normal taxis. The tour covered the Palace moat, grounds and park, from which you could see the Emperor's Imperial Palace and (for security reasons) his son's separate palace; then drove through the Diet Buildings compound; past the Tokyo tower; the Ginza and Roppongi sections, with an intermediate stop at the impressive *Meiji Shinto* shrine. Most Japanese are a combination of Buddhists (during the day), and Shintoists (at night), since Shintoism has few restrictions. They don't appear to be terribly serious about religion. The tour ended at the *Asakusa Kannon* Shinto temple (also very impressive) in our home neighborhood, with its adjoining mad shopping arcade, rivaling the huge almost-mile-long shopping street starting at the Ueno train station and adjoining park (where we had a nice stroll).

We spent the next day- on tour- at Nikko, a 1:40 hour express train ride from *Asakusa* station. Again, as in the ride from the airport, we noted the multiplicity of rice paddies which characterize the countryside, as well as the tight spacing of houses (underlining the shortage of real estate). Nikko is located in the hills by a beautiful lake (*Chuzenzi*) and is a summer resort area, replete with steamer sightseeing/ dining boats, and nice beaches. You go there to see *Toshogu* ("the most famous and magnificent shrine in Japan"- and it lives up to its billing) by winding through a treacherous 48-hairpin-turn road that climbs from 2600 feet to 4100 feet. The shrine is lovely and has a large, beautiful pagoda guarding it. We also saw the 300 foot *Kegon* waterfall and the subsequent *Dragon's Head* cascade. It was a very nice day, albeit rainy in a gentle way. The guide - an elderly gentleman - was voluble and knowledgeable. We returned by train- tired but happy. In summary, the Japanese people were very nice and helpful, and everything was neat and clean and well cared for.

Back to Hong Kong for a brief respite before our week-long foray into China (to be followed by two and a half final days in Hong Kong). Here, as opposed to China), one could drink the tap water, and the beer was very good, too. The school students all wear uniforms. We saw only two American cars!

Our trip to China (see itinerary details, coming) was fabulous, as were all the people who went on the tour with us: a doctor and his wife from Westwood, a couple in the oil business from Saudi Arabia (originally from Pennsylvania and New Jersey, and more lately, Texas), a CPA, and a girl graduate student from southern England, a Londoner now in Saudi hospital administration, with troublesome stories of the treatment of Saudi single women there, but of great salaries and paid travel/vacations as this one, a woman from Indiana who talked a lot, and two young men from Switzerland. The guides varied from great (the first one – alas, it went downhill from there, but still adequate) to unenthusiastic. We saw three all-time show-stopper sites: The Great Wall, the amazing terra cotta folks in Xi'an, and the picturesque unusual mountains by the river Li out of Guilin. Unfortunately, you have to be there to really appreciate them. In Beijing, Tiananmen Square and the huge (Hermosa Beach could fit inside) Forbidden City are also very memorable- but are not the ultimate reasons you should take this trip. Let's start at the top:

Our first taste of China came in Guilin. We got there at night and stayed at the first rate Holiday Inn, being forewarned not to drink the water in China. In the morning, we noted the paucity of cars (and this is a big - 2 million? - city) and the incongruous frequency of distant insistent horn blowing. We also saw the importance of the bicycle for going to business, taking up to 2 kids sitting in back to school, transporting cargo or people in built-in two wheel truck bed contraptions. The bike traffic makes crossing the street hazardous, especially when there was no separate bike road (notice I did not say "path" as this would not be descriptive of the system). We had a western style buffet breakfast and were off to the Li River - along with about 30 (my guess) similar two-deck shallow water boats that proceeded in a seemingly endless stream. We had maps which pointed out the main sights along the way and were helped by our

guide. The scenery was breathless -more so because of the misty wet day. The saw-tooth-like mountains were formed as the ocean receded and ate away the more soluble limestone features. There is probably no similar show in the world. If you don't believe me, I'll send you (or come see) my tape – which turned out excellently. Another outstanding site in Guilin is the very beautiful large *Reed Flute* cave - perhaps as grand as *Carlsbad Caverns*, and even made more beautiful by the fanciful use of colored lighting. Were it not for the *Carlsbad Caverns*, this cave would be reason enough to go to Guilin. We started our week long routine of eating Chinese food twice a day, which except for a special dim-sum blowout that we paid extra for in Xi'an, soon made us chop-stick experts, but now longing for a little more variety in food ethnicity. The 'Chinese' was excellent and much like you get at the restaurant down the street.

U.S. CHINA TRAVEL SERVICE

ITINERARY FOR

MR. BRODSKY ROBERT FOX, MRs. BRODSKY PATRICIA WESS TOUR CODE: 95-KI.-0514C

MAYI4 SUN

HONG KONG/GUILIN

YOU'LL LEAVE FOR GUILIN TODAY. PLEASE KINDLY CHECK IN AT 1720PM AT C. AAC COUNTER, HONG KONG INTERNATIONAL AIRPORT. UPON YOUR ARRIVAL IN GUILIN, YOU'LL BE TRANSFERRED TO HOLIDAY INN GUILIN.

MAY15 MON GUILIN

HAVE BREAKFAST AT THE HOTEL. ENJOY A FIVE-HOUR LI RIVER BOAT TRIP DOWNSTREAM TO YANGSUO WHERE YOU WILL SEE THE BEAUIFUL

SCENERY ALONG IT. LUNCH WILL BE SERVED ON ROUTE. DINNER INILL BE SERVED AFTER RETURNING TO GUILIN BY COACH.

MAY16 TUE GUILIN/BEIJING AIR
HAVE BREAKFAST AT THE HOTEL. SIGHTSEETNG INCLUDES REED FLUTE CAVE, PILED FESTOON HILL, ELEPHANT TRUNK HILL AND A VILLAGE. LUNCH AND DINNER ARE SERVED IN GUILIN. AFTER HAVING DINNER, , FLY TO BEIJING, THE CAPITAL OF THE PEOPLE'S REPUBLIC OF CHINA. UPON ARRIVAL IN BEIJING, YOU'LL BE TRANSFERRED TO HOLIDAY INN LIDO.
MAY17 WED BEIJING
HAVE BREAKFAST AT THE HOTEL. A FULL DAY SIGHTSEEING IN THE CAPITAL OF CHINA INCLUDES THE GREAT WALL AND THE MING TOMBS. ENJOY AN ACROBATTC SHOW. LUNCH AND DINNER ARE SERVED DURING THE VISIT.

MAY18 THU BEIJING
HAVE BREAKFAST AT THE HOTEL. AN EXTENSIVE SIGHT SEEING INCLUDES THE FORBIDDEN CITY, TIANANMEN SQUARE, THE SUMMER PALACE. LUNCH WILL BE SERVED AT A LOCAL RESTAURANT TO TASTE THE FAMOUS PEKING DUCK DINNER THIS EVENING AT ONE OF THE RENOWNED RESTAURANTS.

MAY19 FRI BEIJING/XIAN AIR
HAVE BREAKFAST AT THE HOTEL. VISIT LAMA TEMPLE IN THE MORNING. LUNCH IS SERVED IN BEIJING BEFORE TAKING A FLIGHT TO XIAN. UPON YOUR ARRTVAL IN XIAN, YOU'LL BE TRANSFERRED TO THE GRAND NEW WORLD HOTEL. IF TIME PERMITS, YOU'LL VISIT THE CITY GATE AND THE BIG WILD GOOSE PAGODA. DINNER IS SERVED AT A LOCAL RESTAURANT.

MAY20 SAT XIAN
HAVE BREAKFAST AT THE HOTEL. SIGHTSEEING FOCUSING ON XIAN, THE LARGEST CTTY IN NORTHWEST CHINA AT THE QIN SHI HUANG

MAUSOLEUM, MUSEUM OF TERRA COTTA WARRIORS & HORSES, BANPO MUSEUM, HUA QING HOT SPRINGS RESORT, VISIT A FACTORY MANUFACTURING TERRA COTTA WARRIORS. LUNCH IS SERVEDM DURING THE VISIT. AFTER DINNER AT A RESTAURANT, YOU'LL ENJOY THE IMITATIVE TANG DYNASTY CHOREOGRAPHY PERFORMANCE THIS EVENING.

MAY 21 XIAN XIAN/HONG KONG AIR
HAVE BREAKFAST AT THE HOTEL VISIT THE SHAANXT PROVINCIAL MUSEUM. DEPART FOR HONG KONG AFTER HAVING LUNCH.

THE RIVER LI

Beijing, the Capital of China, is a big (~12 million) city that is flat and inland, with mountains to the west. The main government buildings are on one edge of *Tiananmen* Square. City dwellers are allowed only one child; farmers 2. There is a big business in putting girl babies up for foreign

adoption. It has surprisingly few clusters of significant high rise buildings - but we are told this is changing. Compared to Guilin, there are lots of cars and many fancier type bikes, such as mopeds and a motorized tractor front end of a bike which is loosely attached to a cart with the driver sitting on the cart steering with handlebars and operating a throttle.

As in Guilin, we made a mandatory tour stop at a Chinese clinic which specialized in herbal medicine - with Doctors acting as pitchmen. They had one cure (Old #2) which promised to correct all my ailments - lower back pain, indigestion, impotence, warts, etc. - but Patti wouldn't let me buy any (it was expensive at 15 pills a day!). In addition to the tour stops noted on the itinerary, we also visited a factory that manufactured lovely "*Cloisonne*" ceramic pottery (copper wire-net based) that varied from small to full sized genie proportions; a Chinese "Friendship" store - strictly for foreigners; dinner featuring Peking (ie, Beijing) duck - put in a soft "taco-like" shell with moo-goo sauce and other goodies (it was good, but don't go all the way to China to try it), and a wonderful Chinese acrobatic show as only they can do it.

THE GREAT WALL

But, the Great Wall - its size, seemingly infinite length, and majestic surroundings seem like a pathway both into the past and towards the future. It is a stunner! You're simply not prepared for it, even though you've seen pictures. Another Beijing highlight was the reunion with a friend I had not seen for 15 years. Mr. Zong Shaolu was a visiting scientist that I took on at Iowa State University in the late 70's. He spent 2 years in Ames and returned to his job in the Chinese Guidance and Control Institute. He told me he was responsible for the control system of the Chinese "Long March" launch vehicles and is well known for this and other work. He said that he must retire in two years (at age 63) - by law- and is unhappy about this. In summary, people are not sure what is in store for them when the old man (i.e. Mao) dies. There will be a mild power struggle and probably reform will continue. We never got a feel of any communistic oppression - in fact Mom and Pop enterprises abound- but we certainly did not see beneath the skin.

Xi'an - an ancient walled city that was the capital of several dynasties was our last stop in the PRC. In the surrounding areas one sees the very large funeral mounds that the Emperors and their families were buried in - half under ground and half above ground (reminding one of the pyramids and pharaohs). By far the most sensational (i.e., breathtaking) of these is the Qin (I called it 'Cohen') Dynasty mausoleum guarded by the hordes (estimated eventually to be about one thousand) of terra cotta warrior folks – mostly spearmen, archers, as well as many manned horses and carriages - all with different faces, all originally colored (not now, only vestiges of color left), all life size or slightly bigger, all four in a row, and all dedicated to protecting the emperor, his family and concubines forever. Fabulous!! A true *wonder of the world* - and still a lot of excavating to be done (but not by outsiders!).

XIAN

After seeing them, the rest of the tour was good - but not mind blowing. We saw a plant manufacturing terra cotta folks of all shapes and sizes (and bought some to take home), and a fine museum which had many of the weapons that they took away from the soldiers for some mystical eastern reason. We saw the Emperor's multi-pooled spa, with different pools for different ranks of royalty - the best being reserved for the man himself and his concubines. In fact, in both Japan and China, we got the distinct impression that concubining is where it's at! They had their own palaces and nursemaids and were obviously high up on the food chain.

Xi'an has a bell tower pagoda right in the center of the walled city (to ring in the new day) and a smaller drum tower pagoda hard by to drum in sunset. Our China venture ended with viewing a beautiful pageant in a night club, with a next morning visit to a historical museum (not overwhelming), and thence, for the 3rd time back to Hong Kong, immortalized (only a few of you will know this) by the late Hoagland Carmichael's "*Hong Kong Blues*" *('Dis am de story of a very unfortunate culud man which got 'rested down in old Hong Kong'*, etc). And so, back to California.

SIC TRANSIT GLORIA ORIENTALIS

Chapter 7

ISRAEL / JORDAN - WINTER 1998

(with stops on the way in the East and Germany)

For the record breaking second year in a row, we were out of the country for the holiday season, and consequently unable to send the usual timely holiday greetings cards which help keep in contact with our many friends and well wishers. And, again, this summary of our news, which should reach you while the Sheik and Mrs. Sheik are still celebrating the last available holiday of the year, will hopefully and painlessly tell you of our present status and plans for the New Year.

We started our year-end foray of travel on November 7, 1997, and returned to the USA from the Middle East on December 15, but left almost immediately for Santa Fe to spend the holiday with all of our immediate family, except for the Eastern Brodsky's. We returned on Dec. 29 and have been recovering ever since. Our first stop in the East was in Swampscott, Mass. to celebrate the first birthday of our only girl (out of 6) grandchild, Emily Ann, who was on the brink of starting to walk (now accomplished, to the chagrin of Kobe, the local 130 pound Akita hund, who she is now tormenting despite the obvious fact that he could swallow her in one gulp). Son Jeffrey has just changed jobs; now distributing microchips directly from manufacturers, rather than through a large middleman distributor organization. He made this change for a large increase in earnings but is finding he has less leisure time. Having been swimming in the ocean in Israel the week before, the snow in Massachusetts was a big change - but we were prepared because of our earlier 10 days in November in Germany, before we flew to Israel. In Deutschland, we were hosted by friend, Gretel Schmitt, who lives in the lovely town of Esslingen, near Stuttgart. We have known her 94 year old mother, her daughter Betty, and her sister Hanne for many years. We enjoyed a cold but *Sound of Music*- like hiking outing and lunch at an Inn in the Swabish Alps and a truly gemutlich birthday party mit singin' und bier trinkin' for Hanne. We then visited out dear "adopted" children, now the parents our two German grandchildren, Marina and Peter; the Familie Damm, in their new home in Aachen. Gudrun and Yochen Damm had spent their honeymoon with us in Hermosa.

They showed us the great cathedral and the adjacent office buildings from which Charlemagne ran the Holy Roman Empire and ran the Crusades. We took a side trip to Cologne to see its magnificent Cathedral. I noted a Dixieland jazz venue in the old downtown area. On the train ride back to Stuttgart, we stopped overnight in Heidelberg and saw our friends, the Klagers. We had dinner with them and an Israeli professor friend and his wife (on sabbatical from the Technion) in an old inn (the Sonne) in Neckargemunde (on a mountain top above Heidlberg). Then, on Nov. 22, once more out of the cold and back to warm, beautiful Haifa.

We stayed in Haifa with cousins Susan and Dick Rosenberg and, having 'smuggled' pumpkin pie makings in, prepared for a Thanksgiving dinner. The US fleet was in, so we had a young Alabaman naval officer from a helicopter attack ship for dinner, along with another old friend, Rose Shulman, whose late husband, an Annapolis graduate, had been the first admiral of the Israeli fleet, and the couple (the Abelson's-originally from Cleveland) from Afula who would be going on the Jordan trek with us and the Rosenbergs.

The trip to Jordan was both pleasant and sensational. The sights were tremendous! Throughout, we were accompanied by a very knowledgeable, young Aquaban who spoke excellent English even though he had never been out of Jordan, plus our car driver. After crossing the Jordan at the Hussein Bridge (about 20 miles from Afula, south of the Sea of Galilee and north of the beginning of the "West Bank"), we visited the ancient well-preserved Roman city of Jerash. It is my belief that there are four major Roman town 'ruins': Bet She'an and Caesaria in Israel, Ephesus in Turkey, and Jerash. By 2010, we had visited all four, and in retrospect it is difficult to say which was the most interesting. Each has its outstanding features. Jerash was exemplary in its very well preserved court-yard – a huge paved field surrounded by 30 foot columns. Its coliseum was still utilized and was still used and was in excellent condition. Several municipal buildings were still standing. As with the others, we were amazed that the Romans were able to do so much with the paucity of building materials that they had on hand. The ruins were clearly on a par with the better known Ephesus ruins in Turkey which we had visited during our 1994 semester at the Technion. We spent the night in Amman (to my surprise, Amman was called Philadelphia in the old days - so it was just like returning home!), and the next morning left on the 3 hour drive south to Petra.

PETRA

We arrived at the Movenpick Hotel near to the entrance to Petra (which Santa Fe grandson Alo later recognized as being the site of an *Indiana Jones* movie). Our guide's van took us to an embarking stable, where we mounted mules for the long walk to the entrance – a narrow slit in the hillside and thence into a narrow (two horses could pass, coming and going) pathway of about 200 yards until we got to the city proper. We spent the afternoon walking an estimated total of about 4 miles. We could have hired a camel or a donkey-drawn 2-person cart - but we preferred to rough it. The narrow (20 feet at the widest, and 100 feet high) enfilade (called the "*Siq*") was walled in by multicolored sandstone cliffs which the sun snaked through - what a sight! It led to the city which itself was surrounded by steep cliffs. An impregnable fortress, operated by folks called *Nabateans* whom the Romans never bothered to subdue since they were key to the East-West trade routes. The *Siq* opened up dramatically on Grecian styled buildings that were carved right into the sandstone cliffs. Again, the colors were varied pastels. It was quite a unique adventure

The plaza to our right was at least a football field size. Think of it as being on a relatively flat 'floor' 100 feet below the lips of a volcanic cone. Petra had been a safe haven (vis-a-vis the Huns or Tatars, or whatever marauders preyed on desert travelers); a rest-stop for caravans that emanated from China and India heading to Istanbul or Cairo. The possibility of a successful attack was nil, once in the compound. The homes of the populace were in large caves cut into the sides of the cliff furthest from the entry-way. They were laid out like apartments – with bedrooms, dining rooms and living rooms – all hogged out of the rock. All that was missing were windows (we didn't get a feel for the toilet situation).

Near the entry way were the fairly ornate main municipal buildings: City Hall, the Court House, schools, the library and other municipal buildings and 'hotels' for the travelers. Strewn around the plaza were restaurants, Bar-B-Q pits, tea(?) houses, bazaars, etc. The insides of the municipal buildings were fancy and decorative. They must have required years to construct. It's one of those places you have to see to believe. The following day, on the way back to our hotel and sightseeing tour of Amman, we visited Mt Nebo, where Moses saw the Holy Land and may be buried. Amman, itself, is a modern and seemingly prosperous city. It has a huge (8000 capacity) Roman coliseum right in the smack of downtown, and has various curio shops, such as the one which tried to sell us both gorgeous traditional Arabic costumes. It was a shop founded by then Queen Noor, with profits going to charity.

THE SHEIK AND MRS. ARABY
IN QUEEN NOOR'S SHOP

Back in Haifa, we next hosted the Brooks from Swampscott (Arnold and I went to grad school at NYU together in the late 40's) on a promised 6-day whirlwind tour of Israel. By constantly moving, we managed to "do" Haifa, Jerusalem, Tiberias and the nearby Christian holy sites on the Sea of Galilee, Zefat, Acco (Acre), the Golan Heights, Caesarea, Rosh Ha'niqra and a national monument Tsippouri (new to us - another Roman/Crusader ruin).

We barely had returned to the USA when we left for Santa Fe for the holidays. We rented a van for us, son David

and friends, and our two grandsons from Bolinas. A good time was had by all - and all of the above has been well documented by our trusty camcorder. Now, we'll lay low 'til a mid-March trip to Florida, where I am scheduled to give my last 3~day Remote Sensing seminar.

Chapter 8

A MONTH ON THE ROAD - 2000 (FRANCE, GERMANY, ITALY & MASSACHUSETTS)

Planning for the trip began almost a year ago, when my cousin, Louis Burke, - the then fiftyish son of my mother's youngest sister, and his wife decided to organize a Fox family reunion at their newly acquired villa in Cap d'Antibes. The trip, from Sept. 21 to Oct. 17, 2000, took us by air to Paris, by TGV (Train à Grande Vitesse) to Antibes in southern France, by train from Nice to Lugano on the Swiss-Italy border and thence to Stuttgart; from there by train to Heidelberg and Aachen, then by TGV back to Paris from which we flew to Boston to visit son Jeff before returning home to LAX. In what follows, I'll fill in some details, aided immeasurably by notes taken from Pat's usual impeccable daily journal documenting the action.

My Cousin, a New York City-based commodities lawyer, and his wife, Marce, are Francophiles (southern France variety) - they have been spending 2-3 months a year in Antibes. Last year, they decided to establish a more permanent residence there for their eventual retirement and secured a restored farmhouse, turned into a villa, located about half-way south on the cape, two blocks from the Mediterranean close to two popular beaches on the Nice-facing (Eastern) side.

Antibes, the town, itself is also located on the eastern side of the south-jutting cape, about halfway between Cannes to the SW and Nice to the NE, with the equally fashionable town of Juan Les Pins being just SE of Antibes, also at the beginning (South end) of the cape. The town features a large harbor which can provide docking space for all but very large ocean liners. In fact, the size of about seven of the large private liners docked there was mind boggling (Mostly Turkish and British flags)! The inner city is part of an old well- preserved fortress and features a Picasso museum; appropriate because the old boy used to hang around there. The 'Old City' is picturesque, with narrow streets, a covered open-air market place, a large plaza and many boutiques. Fortunately, we arrived at a perfect time! It was the end of the season, but the weather was beautiful, except for one rainy evening and the next morning, and the Sea temperature was warmer than the villa's unheated pool water – just perfect.

The villa is both luxurious and cozy, and the manners and customs were mostly laid back. The grounds are lush with vegetation, but not huge. There are 4 guest bedrooms on the second floor, each with its own bath; one first floor suite with its own Mediterranean-facing balcony; a master suite with ocean facing balcony on the third floor; and a garage with a small bedroom attached. The first floor, in addition to the added-on suite wing, has a huge entry area, flanked on each side by a living room type coffee table set-up; a formal dining area next to the very adequate kitchen/ pantry/laundry, and a TV/stereo room (which broadcasts music throughout the house). The kitchen area also leads on to an outdoor covered poolside patio where we had breakfast and, on the other side, to a back patio where the bar-b-q is located. All in all, everything you would want in your typical Cote D'Azur villa.

The dramatis personae for the week, in addition to our host and hostess and her long time lady friend (also coincidentally from Redondo Beach), who had been there a week before we arrived, and Pat and me, were cousin Nancy Schweiger and her late thirties professional sous-chef son, Robbie, from North Miami, and her older sister, cousin Alyse O'Neill of Naples, Florida. Both sisters are the children of my Mother's next- to- oldest sister, the late Frances Stern[3]; both are dear; and both are widow-wimmen. Alas, Alyse, the 'black sheep' in a family that is traditionally and emotionally of the Democratic persuasion, is hopelessly very right-wing; an active disciple of Phyllis Schlaffly and the equally delectable Rush Limbaugh. But, she is good hearted and not abrasive about her deviation and is therefore a good friend and companion, who perplexedly suffers with resignation what she sees as our apostasy and lack of reality.

But, that's not all! Just before Pat and I arrived, but before our other cousins appeared, our hosts had also been saddled with another set of couples for a week. They were a cousin on his Father's side and a boyhood buddy. We overlapped the night before the new contingent arrived, and one couple returned for a night during our incumbency prior to going home. I imagine our hosts will think twice before the next family reunion at the Cap!

The day usually started around the breakfast table at around 9:30. I generally watched a bit of the Olympics being broadcast in real time over the Eurosport channel before the gang gathered. Summer clothes were the order of the day. Around 11, we generally took off for the day of sightseeing. Depending on whether our host, (who could conduct his business via phone and fax/email) and/or his wife and her friend came along as guides, we either used our or Alyse's rental car, both of which held five, or caravanned in two cars. Normally the day ended back at

---

3 Whose husband was the uncle of our equally dear and oft-times Israeli visit sponsor, cousin Susan Stern Rosenberg of Haifa.

the chateau around 5-ish, with a cocktail hour and, for me, a swim in the pool to maintain my magnificent body in spite of the food. The latter was generally delicious, starting with the European style breakfasts served up by our hostess, lunches at brasseries while 'on the road', and concluded by late hour lush (and expensive, if eating out, despite the unusually favorable 7 & 1/2 Francs - to - the - Dollar exchange rate) dinners. One night, our hosts arranged for a semi-formal (i.e., no short pants) dinner to be prepared by Jean Luc, a local (American) master Chef. The fish dish he prepared was sumptuous, but both Pat and I felt that a later dinner prepared by Robbie (shrimps and scallops) was superior. On our final night, at a restaurant at the nearby beach, we had a whole sea bass, which had been prepared by entombing it in a thick salt coating and baking it in a hot oven. Tres delicieux!

Jean Luc also starred in an incidental social drama, which proved an eye~opener in two ways to Cousin Alyse. On the evening previous to the Jean Luc dinner, she inadvertently bumped into the corner of a swing-open window on her way up the steps and put a gash in her forehead that obviously required stitches. Louis, Jean Luc (who was reconnoitering in preparation for his dinner night), and I took her to the local hospital, where they only required her name and home address and immediately sent her to emergency. Fifteen minutes and five stitches later we were on our way back to the chateau. Alyse murmured with incredulity, "So this is how Socialized Medicine works?" she also noted that all her attendees were women, and at first she mistook the Doctors for nurses. They later sent her a bill for $132.50, all up!

Except for a hoped-for visit to St. Tropez (we had been there 30 years ago when we lived in Paris), we did all the right tourist things and inhaled just the proper amount of culture to prevent superciliousness. To top it off, cousin Alyse and I took in an afternoon at the local (*Sandy*) beach, where the water was great and half of the women were bare-breasted (the brazen hussies! Can you imagine!). During the week, we accomplished the following prime time sightseeing:

- A complete go-round of Cap d'Antibes; the big harbor with the marinas for the huge yachts and many sailboats; the quaint partially walled 'Old City', with its covered outdoor market; its large plaza, with the old Cathedral, the Picasso museum; the public and pay beaches; the grand hotels including the Cap (where Alyse wanted to go if only for a $5 cup of coffee, but we never made it) and the Belle Rive, where we had dinner one evening under the stars hard by the water; the fabulous super market, 'Carre Four'; the light house - purportedly one of the most powerful on the sea - and its adjoining Chapel with a gorgeous view of the sea towards Nice; and the adjoining tourist town of Juan Les Pins with its casino and disco action.
- A day trip to Monaco, garnished by the lovely drive there along the Bas Corniche (sea level road). We had not been there for 30 years. Then, you could drive your car up to the level of the palace but could not see inside the palace. Today, it is vice-versa. We had to park in a huge structure, which had impossible to follow signs on the way out, making us go down and up about 5 levels until we found the exit. But, in exchange, the palace is open to guided tours, by language persuasion preference. We saw a lovely painting of the royal family and a bust and a painting of Princess Grace, whom I had met- in all her ~ 21 year old model glory- circa 1950 at my friend's sister's wedding in Philadelphia, along with young Frank

Sinatra, who sang at the reception after the formal ceremony.

- We drove by the Casino and the new Convention Center and along the periphery of the medium sized harbor (seen best, in a great view, from the high Palace level). We returned, somewhat late in the afternoon, via the Peage (toll road), which gobbled up Francs every few kilometers. I put on one of my famous snits when we pulled off at the correct place, but mysteriously ended up back on the freeway to face another toll booth at the Juan Les Pins exit.
- Some of our best trips, usually made with our hostess as tour guide, were sallies into the neighboring towns situated in the hills above Antibes, Cannes, and Nice, all nearby. Thus, we saw the old town of Mougins situated high on a shaved-off hill top with its nearby pottery plant; the quaint tourist (pottery and tschotkes) town of Villauris, where we had a nice lunch, waiting for the 2 pm opening of the nearby Renoir home, itself near Haute Cagnes; the big glass works plant in Biot; the ancient town of Vence with its winding alley-ways; and the sensational walled city of St. Paul de Vence, with its castle, narrow winding boutique and gallery-crammed streets, and Bocce Ball action in front of the Hotel de Ville. I was advised by our NYC Cousin Jane, who attends the Cannes film festivals, to look up the proprietor of a gallery there, but alas, left her instructions in the car and missed the connection.
- Jane had also suggested visits to the Chagall museum in Nice and touted the little town of Villefranche as superior, but, like the hoped-for visit to St. Tropez, we just ran out of time and energy. Instead, we spent a morning in Cannes, walking through the high rent district near the 'Palais' where the film festival takes place, and viewing the waterfront

and beaches (sandy, unlike Nice's pebble beaches). It started to rain, but we had a wonderful lunch at a covered outdoor brasserie. The intention was to get some Lire for our cousin's week in Florence, but the rain precluded this - with results to be covered later.

- As noted, we did get a fair amount of 'Kultur'. Renoir's home and garden near Cagnes - where he spent his last days - gave you a real feel of his working realm. On the outskirts of Vence was the beautiful chapel that Matisse designed and donated many charcoal sketches to; and the Leger museum, built near Biot by his widow, was quite marvelous and colorful. His works at the site were both indoor paintings and outside tiles and sculpture.

Suffice it to say, we greatly enjoyed the ambiance of the Cote D'Azur, and believe that our cousins will be very happy when (and, if,) they retire there. We spent some of our last day getting ready for our next leg of the journey. The next morning, the five visiting cousins were to leave on the same late morning train out of Nice, and our host, with two of their three resident cats, was heading back to NYC out of the Nice airport in mid-afternoon. Logistics suggested that we turn in our car one day later than contracted for and at the Nice train station, rather that the gas station in Antibes - 10 miles away – where we had picked it up and where we were supposed to return it. Our host would drop off Alyse's car at the airport, where we had picked it up. This precluded a separate trip by his wife in their car. I give this detail because nothing worked out well: Although I had made arrangements with Hertz for our car (at the quoted additional cost of 500 francs ($67)), 1 had a bill for $336.64 waiting for me when I arrived home and am presently in negotiation, looking forward to yet another small claims court story for my "Annals of Law" chapter in my *A Pilgrim*

Muddles Through book. Later that day, Louis was denied permission to carry both cats with him, necessitating an emergency call to his wife to come pick up the other cat. She later returned to NYC with both cats by the simple expedient of only declaring one of them.

As we left France heading for Genoa, another adventure betook Alyse, Nancy and Robbie who were heading for Florence; little realizing that its name was really Firenze and that Lire were required as the coin of the nonce. As the train neared Genoa, I got a frantic summons from Robbie and company, who were two cars ahead of us. The conductor was telling them, in Franglais, that their travel agent had incorrectly booked them via Milano, an over two hour detour. He was advising them to get off at Genoa and get the train to Pisa and then Florence. They were frantic, because they would lose their seat reservations and would have to twice change trains. I tried to calm them down and reassure them that it was a no-brainer. We watched them walking down the quai at Genoa and had the sinking feeling that, not having any Lire and not even knowing the right name for their destination (both my fault), they —like Charlie on the MTA — were destined to ride the rails of Europe forever. We worried about them the whole rest of the trip, but when we called them on return, found that they had encountered an experienced American lady who was also going their way, and had had no problems.

We arrived at Lugano about 4 pm after a very pleasant ride through the foothills of the Alps. Lago Lugano is the middle lake, between Lago Maggiore (which has to be pronounced using all fingers of your right hand making an upward-facing cone which you move up and down at high frequency as you stretch out the word, Mah- gee-orrr- eeee) and Lago Como; the major lakes of the famous Italian northern lake district. The town of Lugano is actually in Switzerland (we came equipped with Swiss Francs - not as favorable vis-a-vis the dollar as French Francs) and Italian is the local language. The setting is right out of a post card — simply gorgeous! It was overcast and rainy all the time we were there, but the clouds were puffy and sitting about half way up the mountains which surround the lake — Wunderbar! Our hotel, the Excelsior, was located at the edge of the lake across the street and midway along the promenade that borders the water. We had an adventure finding it:

The taxi from the train station could not deliver us to the door, as the streets were blocked. We had come (Sunday, Oct. 1) at the last hours of an annual weekend fiesta celebrating the grape harvest. The narrow street paralleling the blocked main street next to the shore promenade path was jam-packed with vending stands and hordes of people. The 'smart' boutiques remained open and it was just like Chinese fire drill. The cab left us off the inland side of the action street and told us the hotel was "twenty meters down the street". Towing our bags, we cut through the crowd and walked along the blocked main waterside road. We shortly passed a hotel with a big vertical sign that said, "Albergo Hotel" and, forgetting that the Italian word for hotel is 'Albergo", forged on. Finally, I asked a waiter in a streetside cafe, "Dove Hotel Excelsior?" Of course, he pointed at the Albergo Hotel sign, underneath which was a horizontal sign "Excelsior' and we sheepishly checked into a fine room with a fifth floor balcony overlooking the water.

The season was already over for tourists, but you could see why Lugano is one of the big resort towns during the summer. The water is probably too cold for swimming, but the lake appears ideal for boating and water sports and tanning at the beach. It won hands down over the Isola that we had stayed at in Maggiore a few years earlier. We left the next mid-day on the train to Stuttgart. The ride, through the Alps via Zurich was beautiful. Lugano was a good stop to leisurely wind down and get ready for the next segments of our journey.

We stayed in Esslingen, a lovely town east of Stuttgart, in the apartment of the mother of our friend, Gretel Schmitt, a frequent visitor to our beach homes. She is the niece of my late former nurse who lived at our house in Philadelphia from my first year until I went away to college at age 16, and later lived with us in Iowa. Gretel had just returned from a week's vacation with friends on an island beach named, "Sylt". It is located in the North Sea near Hamburg, and loved it!

Gretel's Mother, Oma (who once visited us in Hermosa Beach) is now 94 and recently had to move to a 'old age' home as she was no longer capable of living alone. Her apartment remains in limbo as her family does not want to preclude the possibility of her making a comeback. This is a heart wrenching state of affairs; Oma is still lucent and does get around with a walker, but the place she is in, as nice and caring as it is, still reminds us of the 'Elephant's graveyard' in the old Tarzan pix. Pattie and I both hope we don't end up in similar circumstances, unless we can still pursue simple things like watching TV, reading, or continuing to write epics such as we now do.

We had a quiet time there, visiting Oma and Gretel's daughter, Betty; shopping for presents for the rest of the trip; doing our accumulated laundry; visiting with Gretel's friend, Gisela, who had also visited us and shared the wild and harrowing 'Space Ride' with me at Disneyland; and walking and mild sight-seeing. The latter included watching a very interesting Glider launching operation from a grass field above Esslingen. A single truck, located about 250 yards down the runway and equipped with a large rotating drum reeling up the launcher cable did the job. At release of the cable, the gliders were around 500 feet high at an angle of ~45 degrees. As they disengaged the cable, they nosed down and started on their journey, depending on thermals and upward moving air from the valley below to get them back to the field. It was a pleasant stay, and we look forward to Gretel's next visit to the USA, as soon as she is free.

As an aside, we noted that the idea of Halloween has been actively adopted in Germany (and to a lesser extent in France). The same hype as we see here, with pumpkins, goblins and witches. We also noted a special showing of the "Rocky-Horror-Picture-Show" on Freitag, 27 Oktober, 2000 in Monschau, with costume-wearing suggested. Another American cultural triumph!

On Friday, on our way to our next stop, Aachen, we had brunch with our friends Max and Nieta Klager in Heidelberg. Max is an Emeritus Professor at dear old H.U. whose mother was a friend of my nanny. He is an author and the sponsor, promoter, and documentarian of a now well - known group of handicapped artists. He had just returned from Austria, where he received an award and medal from its very President for the art appreciation classes he has been conducting for a large Foundation in support of the handicapped. He still teaches at the University.

It was the usual pleasant ride from Heidelberg to Cologne, mostly along the Rhine, with its many castles and busy riverboat action, enhanced this time by a glimpse of the beginning of the fall foliage, combined with overcast skies. Aachen is the home of our adopted children, the Damm's; Gudrun and Yochen, and our adopted grandchildren, Marina (12) and Peter (8), then. We first met in the early 80's, when Gudrun was a law student studying to be a Judge, which she later became (but now, is a lawyer concerned mostly with Medical/Pharmeceutical law). We then decided to become pen pals; she writing me in English and I writing her in Deutsche. Needless to say, she now speaks and writes English beautifully, while nobody except Pat (and Gretel, God bless her- she acts as my interpreter) understands my German. But, for some reason, Marina - who has begun to study English at school (we brought her a Harry Potter in English so she can read it using her cousin's German version) - and Peter, who hears English spoken at home occasionally - both understand me most of the time (or pretend to?).

Yochen is Comptroller for the huge Swedish international electronics giant, Ericsson, whose official company language is English; he being quite fluent, although a native Aachener. Gudrun and Yochen honeymooned in California, using our place as a base, and visited us again a couple of years ago. This time, we asked the kids to come next year bringing their parents, promising our Disneyland version (they have been to the one near Paris) and Universal Studios, etc. They can't wait!

We received our usual loving welcome from die Familie Damm and, after catching up on the news and supervising Peter while he built three "gummyband"—launched gliders which we then successfully and gleefully flew (the start of his aerospace career?) in an adjoining horse pasture, spent most of the next day on a lovely excursion: Aachen is located at Germany's most Westward area, a three-corners position where the Holland, Belgium, and Germany boundaries meet. For our day's outing, we drove South into a lovely rolling hills, mostly agricultural, region called Eifel. A large river, the Rur, flows there and, by damming, forms three large lakes, the Rursee, Obersee, and Urftsee; all very sylvan and picturesque. The Rursee, where we first stopped to observe the sail boats and skip rocks, features two large sight-seeing boats. We walked along the shore at the post-card town of Rurberg, and then visited the wonderful narrow-streeted tourist town of Monschau, with its impressive glass factory. The Rur runs swiftly through the town, and the houses perched on each side of the bank reminded me of a similar situation in Alaska (Ketchican?). We even were treated to a fly-fisherman in waders. We love the whole Damm family, if you'll pardon the pun, and — as always- hated to leave them as we boarded the TGV on Sunday for Paris. On the train, we met and talked to an interesting multi-named (Godefroid MARUME MulumE) Geneva-based Counsel from the Congo/Zaire embassy, who spoke fluent French (official language of the Congo), very good English and 4 native dialects: Swahili, Mbote, Tshiluba, and Kikongo. He said that English is becoming popular there, and you can see why.

In Paris, we have been staying at the hotel (Hospitel) located within the city hospital (l'Hotel de Dieu) right next to Notre Dame – a wonderful convenient and comfortable location at a reasonable price, with a window that looks right at the Cathedral and resonates when the bells ring. Shortly after we had settled in, we got a call from my former Paris Office Manager, Gudrun Ladoire, who told us that she and husband Claude were not able to pick us up because their dog was dying of cancer, and could not stand the 60 mile trip to the train station from their house in the country. They invited us there, but because of the arrival of other friends, we could not go. Instead, we extracted their solemn promise to visit us in 2001. On what would be our only night alone in Paris, we naturally went to eat at our old stamping ground, the *Entrecote* at Pt. Maillot, whose fixed menu (steck-frites with mustard sauce) and great taste has not changed a whit in the 30 years that we have been eating there.

The next morning (Monday), we got a call from my old Navy and continuing buddy, Tommy Carrig, who with his wife Nancy have been living in Copenhagen for over 30 years. They had, indeed, made the trip (their confirming letter arrived in California after we had left, so we did not think they would come) and were in a nearby hotel. We had not seen them for a few years (a 1996 rendezvous in Paris, as I recall) and we were not sure how well Tommy had recovered from a severe stroke he suffered a year ago. It turned out that he was still recovering from the effects of the stroke; his stamina was such that we had to make rest stops when we walked; but otherwise he retained his sense of humor and laid back life philosophy which always endeared him to me. Alas, he has had to give up on some of his hobbies, such as taking an occasional toke, but is even philosophical about this. None-the-less, had we known of the sacrifice they made in coming, we would have arranged to visit them in Denmark, instead.

We spent a leisurely day, first doing some shopping at the major department store near the City Hall, the *BHV* (pronounced 'Bay, Asch, Vay'), the bazaar at the Hotel de Ville, which has one of THE great hardware departments in the civilized world. After lunch, we headed, by bus, for a new exhibition featuring Mediterranean impressionist artists, at the Grand Palais. This was a new experience for Pat and me; believe it or not, in all the time we lived in Paris we had never taken a bus, usually using only the Metro. We found that the same 'billet' that works on the Metro also works for the bus. When we got to the Museum, we found that the line was huge and slow moving, so we decided to give it up. We had trouble finding a cab (it was drizzling slightly), which we had decided to take to save Tommy from more walking. When we finally hailed a live one, it could only take 3 passengers. It turns out that there are now two sizes of cabs in the city; a small one like the one we hailed and was used by Tommy, and the even more difficult to find larger ones. Patti and I decided to walk back - and the two plus mile walk proved to be a good one. We rested in our room and in heavy rain (using a parapluie borrowed from the Hospitel) met the Carrigs and ate dinner near their hotel in the Latin Quarter.

The next morning, after the usual petit dejeuner served in our room, we decided to walk down the Boul'Mich to see how far the Hotel Madison, where our friends from Swampscott, Mass., the Brooks, were due to check in around noon, was from the Carrig's hotel. It proved to be within Tommy's walking range, which we duly reported back to them. At the hotel, a typical Parisian French repartee took place with the concierge (I had forgotten about the snobbishness of Parisians insofar as their language is concerned). In my best French, I asked the concierge, "S'il vous plait, est-ce que Les Brooks de Boston sont arrive cependant?" She looked at me quizzically, and in English - with a sneer - said, "What language are you speaking?" Helas! Les temps ne change pas!

We went back to the Madison after reporting our distance findings to the Carrig's and met the Brooks at their hotel (they said the concierge had actually mellowed in her dealings with them since their previous visit). By pre-arrangement, we met the Carrigs nearby and had an excellent and filling lunch at a favorite restaurant of Nancy's. The Brooks, Arnold and Lenore, had not seen Tom since our mutual New York days in the late 40's, when Arnie and I were grad students at NYU. We all rested in our respective hotel rooms after lunch, with the Brooks resigning for the day to catch up on their jet lag.

Patti and I pulled ourselves together around 5 pm and took a walk. We wanted to see the recently opened "Musee d'Art et d'Histoire du Judaisme", located nearby in a lovely old (1650) chateau, l'Hotel de Saint-Aignan, at 71, rue du Temple, in the old Marais district. We found it readily, but it was closed for the day. We decided that we would not go back tomorrow, because it might be dangerous. The 'troubles' with the PLO in Israel were at their height, and Jewish structures in France were being bombed. A sad commentary on the world today! On the way back to our room, we passed the newly renovated and re-opened and still gaudily painted Pompidou museum - doing a great business.

That evening we were not particularly hungry, so we brought a bottle of vin rouge and cheese and croissants and took them to Tommy's room. We had a wonderful evening, reminiscing about the old days, the music, and the musicians who shared our lives in the '40's. The next morning, we met the Carrig's and walked to the Luxembourg Gardens, where we enjoyed strolling and sitting in the park, watching the fork lifts bringing in the huge 'crate-planted' trees into a large shelter for the winter. Then, in the Garden's art museum, we saw a panoply of great works which spanned over a 100 years (from 'Bonnard to Monet'), followed by a lunch at a nearby brasserie. Back at our hotel, we called Gudrun to say goodbye and found, sadly, that their dog would be put to sleep the next day before they left for Africa.

We had made a grand plan to all meet for dinner at an excellent sea food restaurant (*Jarasse*) in our old ('69-'70) neighborhood in Neuilly. Lenore wanted to see our former house there and walk in the nearby Bois de Bolougne, and we agreed to meet her in front of the restaurant around 4:30, while Arnold and the Carrig's were to meet us around 7 pm. We took the old #1 Metro line to Pont de Neuilly (where the Seine goes under the Ave. dc Neuilly, now Ave. Charles DeGaulle) and found that the up-escalator ne marche pas. The train level was about a 'mile' below street level, and we immediately knew that Tommy would be hard put to walk up the stairs. We met Lenore, and during our tour decided to try to head off the others and instead meet at the Brook's hotel and eat at their local version of L'Entrecote. The problem was to find a phone to call them. Miraculously, we stumbled upon a phone booth and, with great ingenuity I thought, I found a way to make the calls without a French phone card. I used my MCI card, and it worked!

Arrangements were made and we continued our 'uptown' (I always think of the Champs d'Elysses as North-South, although in reality it is East-West) tour, to Lenore's delight. Quelle Memoires! As an aside, I should mention an ugly fall-out of L'Affaire Escalator. Back at home, I just got my phone bill. Despite paying MCI $8.95 monthly to get low rate overseas phone service, and despite being told by them to always use my calling card when abroad, the suckers charged me $10.16 for each of the less than two minute calls! Naturally, I am in the middle of the protest and will only pay them their quoted overseas French rates. I have already switched to Econophone, a fly-by-night outfit recommended by a chary friend. I am presently waiting for them to send me the tin cans and string but, alas, they don't give frequent flyer miles.

On the Metro back to the Madison, we had to 'fait une correspondance' at *Chatelet*. Here, an earthshaking event took place so quickly that it could not be recorded by the human eye. It was in the middle of rush hour, and the cars were jammed. Pat and Lenore were swept on board by what we think were three teenagers. One effectively blocked me out of view at the door entrance. The other two tried to 'dip' the lady's purses, and in Pat's case almost succeeded in relieving her of her wallet. The one going for Lenore's apparently unzipped the wrong zipper. As the lady's successfully reacted, the three ran out of the door just as it was closing. We are keenly aware of what to look out for now, and will apply this new found skill during our forthcoming jaunt to Rio, where it is reputed that every other person is a famous dip.

The *Entrecote* in the Boul'mich area is just not the same as our favorite 'branch' at Pt. Maillot. It is tonier, less crowded, and somehow not as good, although the menu is identical. Afterwards, we walked back through the great narrow streets of the quarter, saw the full moon over Notre Dame, and said our fond farewell to the Carrig's and Brook's, the latter going on to Berlin and Munich. In the morning, before getting a cab to the airport, we made a last walk through the Latin Quarter and joined the tourists inside the cathedral, a pilgrimage we hadn't done for thirty years. They have cleaned the outside to a lovely white; the inside remains beautiful, too.

We arrived in New England at the very peak of the fall foliage show - which was simply spectacular (just as I remembered it when I used to return to Cornell for the Fall semesters). Son Jeffrey, his wife Lori and girls, Emily Ann (4) and Caroline(1+), (our other five grandchildren are all male) had recently moved to Shrewsbury, about 20 miles West of Boston. Although we had earlier seen their new house while the previous owners were still there, this was our initiation to its decor a la Jeff and Lori. It is a big comfortable house with lots of lawn. We were in one of the 4 second story bed rooms. The first floor features a large comfortable den with a big stone fireplace, in addition to a large (still unfurnished) living room, large kitchen, dining room, and foyer. The bottom floor has a huge den and playing area.

Shrewsbury is near Worcester, the ancestral home of my former Gulfport and Navy Pier (Chicago) Navy buddies, Howard Cheney and Eli Braley. I looked both of them up in the local phone book, which featured Worcester, and sure enough found a Howard Cheney, Jr. I figured he must be the son, but when I called him he turned out to be the original goods. We had a good 55 year reunion over the phone, and he told me that Eli was also still in business.

Our family visit was a pleasant one. Both Lori and Emily Ann are taking riding instruction. Lori wants to get back to jumping, and we watched Emily do her first true posting. We went to a large swap meet, and picnicked by a beautiful local lake. And we watched the rites of pick-up and delivery of Emily to her day school. And, again, we found out how physically hard it is to be a grandparent to two kids, and again decided that having children was only for the young.

We spent 5 days with our family, and were glad to get back home- even with the mountains of mail, phone messages, e-mail messages, and bills waiting for us. We got home on Tuesday. The next day, I was back on the high seas!

Chapter 9

SOUTH AMERICAN ADVENTURES - 2001

Hi Yi, Yi — Yi[4]

A set of unusual circumstances led to our Jan 31 to Feb 22, 2001 South American adventure. In 1989, while I was a Visiting Professor, my best student in the Spacecraft Systems Design course that I was teaching at the *Technion* in Haifa was a girl, Sylvi, from Montevideo, Uruguay. Subsequently, I arranged for her to get a graduate assistantship at USC. When she was awarded her PhD in May 2000, her parents, Leon and Martha, who came here to L.A. to witness the ceremony, stayed at our condo, since we were off on our Panama Canal/Acapulco trip to commemorate my 75th birthday. They kindly offered us a week at their beach chalet in *Punte Del Este*, the Miami Beach of eastern South America, and we decided to grab it up. We were joined by our Iowa State friends and former neighbors in Ames, Don and Donna Newbrough, with whom we had previously shared visits to Israel/Egypt and an 11 day Mexican Riviera cruise. Don was our family lawyer while we lived in Iowa. Donna, his wife, was a retired Dean of Home Economics.

By the luck of the Irish, we stumbled on the world's greatest South American travel agent. Gustavo Barreiro, a native son of Buenos Aires, who arranged an almost perfect 23 day trip for us, including fabulous 'extra's', at a cost of less than $2000 per

4 Hi Yi Yi - Have you ever danced' in the tropics? ------ The gay, romantical, South American way. ("*South American Way*") by Carmen Miranda

person. This included pick up at and delivery to all airports, hotel accommodations with breakfast (except for the week at the beach) as well as various tours and outings which will be described. The trip consisted of 3 days in *Montevideo*, a week in *Punte Del Este*, 3+ days in *Buenos Aires*, 2+ days at *Iguassu Falls*, and 4+ days in *Rio*; plus two long travel days from and back to the land of the Norte Americanos.

Except for the internal flights, our main carrier was United Airlines, and we racked up around 15,000 miles each. We joined the Newbrough's in Chicago, and flew from O'Hare to *Montevideo* via a stop and plane change in *Buenos Aires*. The long flight featured an excellent dinner - an Air France-like menu - with free drinks for the house. A sleeping pill allowed us to arrive in Montevideo rested and with no jet lag, despite the 5-hour time difference from LA (if you look at the map, you'll see that eastern SA is closer to Africa than it is to Mexico). But, before we begin the travelogue, let us comment on the most unexpected aspect of the journey: Now, I'm not quite sure of what prior image we had cooked up for South America -maybe it was one of a mixture of brown-faced Mexico, the Wild West, and Las Vegas strip show girls? Anyway, despite our brief year-ago initial SA venture into downtown *Caracas* on our Panama Canal trip (and this should have made us suspicious of our image since we could not distinguish that part of the city from downtown LA), it turns out that - except for language peculiarities and a lack of Pacific Rim-type faces - you could easily believe you hadn't left the USA. Indeed, Europe is much more "foreign" than anything we saw in South America! The faces, body types, clothing, obvious hopes and aspirations, and general demeanor were indistinguishable from those appearing in any large American city, including the ubiquitous McDonald's everywhere, the malls, boutiques, stores, museums, architecture, and manners and customs. This was surprising to us. On the other hand, English-speakers were the exception, and the only English language newspaper we found in *MV, PDE,* and *BA* was the good old *Buenos Aires Herald*, and it was not available in Brazil. Of course, CNN was on TV everywhere, and there is a separate Espanol-sprechen CNN channel, too.

We arrived on time, around 1 pm local time, at the Montevideo airport, and were met both by a guide, replete with the soon-to-be familiar "Brodsky-Newbrough" sign, as well as by our wonderful hosts, Martha and Leon, who wanted to make sure we got a proper introduction to Uruguay - a country they obviously love. The latitude is about the same as LA's, thus the weather, now approaching the end of summer, was like August at home. The Newbrough's had left behind 10 degree weather in Ames - imagine their delight! Our chauffeured van took us to the very nice 3-star Hotel Lafayette, strategically located in the downtown area, 2 short blocks from the broad main drag, Ave. 18 de Julio (Independence Day). On the way in, I noticed that most restaurants seemed to be named 'Parilla'. I later learned that this meant they had an open fire bar-b-q going, loaded with beef, pork, chicken, and sausages. The South American appetites proved to be huge and their eating hours very late.

We had arrived in Montevideo at a very opportune time. Our first night marked the beginning of an annual two-day Carnivale-like celebration dedicated to the Sea Goddess - a mixture of Christian and African spiritualistic rites participated in by neighborhood and church groups - Black and White. We found that the large Black population descended from African slaves - which I had never been aware of – who were now well integrated into the Uruguayan society. Not so the former indigenous 'Indians' who were pretty well ethnically 'cleansed' in the early frontier days and had essentially disappeared. Leon had arranged for seats for us and their lawyer son, Daniel and his very pregnant wife, Patricia (Rafael was born before we returned home) along the parade route on 18 Julio near our hotel. The parade itself - costumed marchers and floats and bands — lasted over 4 hours and was what I think was a less lavish version of what I imagine the Carnivale in Rio to be. Gustavo had advised us not to be in Rio at Carnivale time; feeling that unless we were willing to carouse all night, it was just too frantic for Alte Cockers. I got a lot of great footage on my camcorder - whose film tape also had pictures, narrated in Spanish by Sylvi, of her just-occupied 'new' house in Manhattan Beach which we planned to show the next evening at her parent's condo.

The parade was colorful and participated in by thousands of people, almost matching the huge crowd that watched along the parade route. We gave up at about 11 pm and fought our way through the crowd to our first Uruguayan dinner. As we expected, meat, especially various cuts of beef, is the big SA favorite. It was a great introduction for the cuisine to follow (*Loma* - thick beef, *Chivito* - a meat sandwich with lots of extras, etc.). Somehow, Patti, who usually is in bed very early, and I, used to dining at or before 6pm, adapted to the new routine of late dinners and midnight-or-later sack-hitting. So we were up and ready the next morning when Leon appeared to take us for a city tour. He covered the main buildings and parks, and the major shopping centers of the city of a million and a half people (half the population of Uruguay). Especially noteworthy was a huge bronze 'statue' depicting an oxen-drawn wagon carrying early settlers. We drove along the *rampla* - the large boulevard that skirts the 'river'. Leon noted 'his' beach, *Pocitos*, in his neighborhood. The *Rio de la Plata*, where it flows by *Montevideo* and then *Punte del Este*, is over a hundred miles wide to the North and should more rightly be called a bay. It remains very wide even a hundred miles inland to the west where it flows by *Buenos Aires*. The water near the shore is slightly brownish from silt, however this does not deter the bathers. It finally officially becomes the Atlantic Ocean about another 85 miles downstream at Punte Del Este. My suspicion is that it must be half pure - half salty at Montevideo.

We had a formal half-day city tour in the afternoon and revisited many of the sights that Leon, a retired Orthopedic surgeon, had shown us in the morning. The new things we saw included a ride through the very impressive suburban 'affluent' district; another outstanding bronze monument; a tour of the old city with some old classical churches and government buildings; ending at the harbor. We then made a visit to the 500 foot 'hill', the *Cerro*, after which *Montevideo* ("I see a mountain") was named, with its harbor-guarding fortress from where we had an outstanding view of the harbor and city. The tour confirmed that in South America, judging from our experience in Venezuela (Simon *Bolivar*) and Uruguay (*Jose Artigas*) and, later, in Argentina (*San Martin*), there are statutes of many 'Men on Horseback'- the liberators of those countries from Spanish rule.

That evening, Leon picked us up and took us to the beach, where the same huge crowd that had been at the parade the night before was now celebrating the second part of the Sea Goddess festival. I dutifully recorded much of the pagan goings-on, which consisted of various candle-lit laying-on-of-hands rites with seers, drummers and singers. Paper boats, with lit candles in them, were launched off shore and floated in. It was very exciting! We were walking back towards the car. I was holding my camcorder in my hand by my side when suddenly it was snatched away by a couple of kids who disappeared into the crowd before I could react. Since I also had a camcorder stolen from me in Israel a year ago, we have decided to go out of the movie-taking business. Our $500 deductible insurance simply can't hack it.

We had late Friday night dinner at Leon and Martha's, with Daniel and Patricia. We learned about Martha's empanadas, a delicious meat-stuffed Uruguayan-version knish, served as an appetizer. She must have spent the day preparing them! We also met the family hund, *Tango*, a friendly large black Lab retriever, who had obviously taken Sylvi's place in the household. Martha, who is an artist, showed us her outstanding tapestry work and confirmed that she was just finishing one as a gift for us. It was now at her school, which she attended twice a week. We had more food — the main course – even though we were stuffed with the empanadas, and finally called it a night around I a.m.

On Saturday, while our hosts drove to *Punta Del Este* to make sure the beach house was ready and stocked, we had a 'free' day in MV. We went to a leather shop (the work is beautiful and the leather soft, but not for California tastes) and then to the beautiful ancient iron-work- constructed Mercado del Puerto at the end of the old city next to the harbor. The market consists of meat and fish stores and many parillas - their wood-fired grills loaded with delicious looking meats, chickens parts, and sausages. We had lunch at the recommended *El Palenque*, outdoors aside the market, then taxied to a nearby plaza where a flea market was taking place. Finally, after making the long walk back to the hotel area, we visited a couple of smart boutiques that Leon had pointed out. We finished the day early by eating hot dogs(!) at a nearby park. We had 'done' Montevideo and were ready for a week at the beach!

Next day, we took a 10am bus for the leisurely two hour ride to *Punta Del Este*, where Leon was to meet us at the bus station. We got our first look at PDE as we got on the rampla from a stop in the city of *Maldonado*, slightly inland. We were on the 'river' side and saw the peninsula and its harbor —all very reminiscent of Miami Beach with its high rise hotels and condos. It looked very hospitable and we became anxious to get there and see it first hand. We were not to be disappointed!

Leon picked us up at the bus station, and miraculously loaded all our baggage in the trunk and on the roof racks of his car, and whisked us off to the "chalette", as he pronounced it. Leon's English is chancy, but Martha's is excellent. Her parents were Lithuanian and moved to Argentina and his moved from Romania to Uruguay; both are now true Uruguayans. The chalet "*Cunatai*" turned out to be a comfortable 3 bedroom house located at the base of the peninsula, equidistant from our favorite 'Bay' (Cinco) beach and the nearest ocean (Papa Charlie's) beach, but not within walking distance if carrying the requisite beach chair/umbrella. No sooner had we arrived than Leon showed us the enormous parilla lunch he had going on the special outdoor fireplace. We noshed on the leftovers for the whole week!

After lunch, Leon took us on a tour of PDE, starting near the bus station whose nearby beach features the fingers of a huge hand sticking out of the sand. First he showed us the nearby local stores and super-mercado mall. We then toured the rampla; drove through the harbor; stopped at the beaches that we would use and met the parking major-domos at each (Leon advised 5 pesos tip—about 50 cents); went through the busy downtown with its many restaurants, boutiques and flea market, past the huge Hilton Hotel, the *CONRAD*, with its big casino; noting that 90% of the cars had Argentinian plates (Tout Buenos Aires!). The beaches are all given numbers (the bay-side beaches up to #39, and the ocean side beaches up to # 40 at *Punte de LaBarra*, the northern end of PDE). The Beaches are also given names, after beachside restaurants or other features, e.g., Cinco beach is '*La Pastora*' and Papa Charlie's is '*Playa Brava*'. We next went to the airport to pick up our rental car. In a week, we would return it to fly from PDE to Buenos Aires. On the way to our chalet, we stopped at several scenic view hills and ports and saw the sensational *CASA PUEBLO* hotel – a pure white part-Moroccan, part-Disneyland castle/edifice located high on a hill above the bay. Our hosts and Tango left us around 5pm, promising to return next Saturday evening to help us get to the airport next Sunday.

The week at PDE was glorious! We stocked up the refrigerator, bought beach chairs and towels and wine (the chalet came with a beach umbrella and bicycles, beer and bottled water — although throughout the trip Pat and I used tap water with no repercussions), found CNN and other English - speaking channels and soon got familiar with the town. After leisurely late breakfasts, we spent relaxing soothing days on the beach, basking in the warm sun (about 85 degrees) and equally warm water; one day on the bay side, the next on the ocean side. Nowhere, alas, were there bare-breasted ladies, even tho' the city fathers had recently approved such (lack of) attire in a blatant attempt to attract more Argentinians and Brazilians. There were, however, scantily covered boobs aplenty and most of the girls —God bless 'em - wore thong bottoms. We managed to surreptitiously take a picture with Don and I on each side of a trio of lovely sandy bottoms. We soon got separated by the traffic. I made a turn a block or two too soon, and we had to painfully retreat our steps. When we finally got to the restaurant, we found that the others had been there and gone, apparently believing we would never make it. We sat down and had a drink, waiting for the others to return. When they didn't, Leon - knowing that we had the only keys to get into the security alerted chalet - went back to house. There he found the group and, in his car, brought them back to the restaurant, where we had a wonderful, but very late meal. All six of us squeezed into his car and made it back home. We watched the colorful fireworks and went to bed exhausted. All went well the next morning, including push-starting the rental car, whose battery had inexplicably died during the night, and we said our sad 'goodbyes' at the airport, paying an unexpected but not large departure fee, and were off to Tangoland.

Even though we were over two hours late, we were greeted by a patient driver at the internal (as opposed to the distant international airport) airport, located in the suburban part of the city along the river bank, and quickly delivered to the Continental Hotel. This turned out to be very nice and strategically located near the Obelisk, the city's main monument. It was located in the middle, lengthwise, of the Avenida de 9 Julio, reputedly the widest street in the world. Indeed, the next day, it took us about 5 minutes (three red light's worth) to cross it. In one direction, towards the harbor, it ends at the Plaza de Constitution and at the other, in the freeway to the east. We parenthetically decided that, based on *MV* and *BA* and the USA, all the important independence days in history must have taken place in July.

Buenos Aires is a huge city with 34 distinctive barrios (neighborhoods). Our half-day tour took us through 7 of them, but these were presumably the most interesting and disparate. The city is modern, somewhat European in feeling in places and very American - feeling in others. Since that same company provided us with guides and vans at all stops, the word must have been out that the women were interested in leather clothing. So our first widespread look at the city occurred when we were picked and whisked of to a 'leather factory'. Pat and Donna showed great restraint in not going for the truly beautiful shirts and skirts that went for around $300. Argentine's Peso was pegged one-for-one with the Dollar, and the latter is freely accepted. Brazil's *Real* was less tightly pegged at around 50 cents, but dollars were also acceptable; and prices were very reasonable in both countries.

The city tour took us through the central district which contained our hotel, as well as many impressive edifices like the pink 'Governor's House" from which the Peron's addressed the unwashed masses from its balcony overlooking the large *Plaza de Mayo*. Also visited were the very classic opera house, the *Teatro Colon*, and the impressive metropolitan cathedral. Next we rode through the Soho-like *Recoleta* district, with its many up-scale high rises and street cafes. We only got a glimpse of the famous cemetery, but would return there the next day, as will be reported. We visited a series of beautiful parks, with rose and Japanese gardens and with boating, facilities, got a look at the high-rent residential districts (e.g., *Palermo*); drove through the *Monserrat* district with its government buildings, through the *San Telmo* district, the home of most of the

Tango Bars and revue halls, until we reached the waterfront *La Boca* district. This is a very colorful neighborhood called '*Caminito*'. The brightly colored houses (reds, blues, greens, and yellows pre- dominated) were generally made of corrugated tin, the only inexpensive building material available at the time for the many Italian immigrants who settled there and worked on the waterfront. Now, it is a picture-book tourist trap - a stop for all the tour buses - with the usual tschotke - laden boutiques, and - for today, at least - a living-statue lady (and dog), adorned in gold.

BUENOS AIRES – LA BOCA (ITALIAN) SECTION

We later taxied to the famous *Recoleta* cemetery district to see a site that is probably unique. The large (and completely subscribed to, I guess) grounds contained a virtual city of houses - mausoleums in this case- one more classy than the other. Beautiful structures, some classic, some ultra-modern, most including a chapel area and all having enough room to hold several generations of the same family. A young guide showed us to Evita's house, almost certainly the one most visited. The Duarte family tomb was nothing special compared to the more affluent personages and the liberators - but the whole history of Argentina was there - an outstanding sight to see!

BUENOS AIRES – CITY CEMETERY – EVITA'S 'HOUSE' 2RD FROM LEFT

On the next day, we were transported to a Gaucho ranch about 20 miles down river. The outing featured a huge parilla lunch, horseback riding for them that were gung-ho, a gaucho museum, and a horseback riding show after the no-holds-barred lunch. The wine flowed like water, and we came to appreciate the indigenous brand called "*Mendoza*" from a section of the country in the northwest, next to Chile. We bused with a group of French people from *Biarritz* who were pleased with my parlez-ing, making up somewhat for the terrible snub I received in Paris earlier this Fall, when a snide concierge asked me, "What language are you speaking"? In passing, let us note that the Uruguayan beer (*Pilsen*), and the Argentinian/Brazilian beer (*Antarctic*) were excellent, and that we confirmed that the appetites of our southern neighbors are phenomenal! The gaucho day was very pleasant and not tiring. In the evening, we walked along a main 'walk street' (*Avenida Florida*) and found an outstanding English oyster bar for dinner (*Clark's*). We had time to walk around the various shopping streets, and made a crusade of trying to find riding crops for Donna's grandchildren. We finally were successful, and - on the way – enjoyed several arts and crafts shops. Prices were generally lower than in the US.

Our package also included an evening (dinner and a 3 hour show) at a *San Telmo* tango palace, the *La Ventana*. We sat at a table for eight, with a widower from Germany (Donna and I got a chance to flaunt our Deutsche-sprechen without giving him obvious indigestion), and a family of three from Chile who spoke a little English. The show was marvelous (though a bit too long) and included music, singing, and much tango dancing. When we left for *Iguassu*, we felt we had gotten a good feel for the city, even though we missed many of its barrios and did not schmooze around in the cafes, as is de rigueur to do.

After paying another reasonable departure fee from *BA*, we arrived at the Argentinian airport that serves *Iguassu* (or, *Iguazzu*) around 2pm, after a one and a half hour flight. We were met by our guide, who skillfully got us through the border crossing into Brazil (*Iguassu* is located near the joint borders of Argentina, Brazil, and Paraguay, about 800 miles west-southwest of *Rio*) with a minimum of fuss, and no entry fee since we had already paid $60 each for a visit visa. We were taken to the Panorama Hotel, about 10 miles from the

Falls and on the outskirts of the main Brazilian town, *Foz de Iguassu*. The hotel was a gem, featuring a large pool with a poolside bar, and many amenities. One of the latter was a lovely Chilean bathing beauty with whom that devil, Don, struck up a conversation (she was an English teacher). Donna, in the sack with a slight headache, never knew!

"Breathtaking" is a vastly inadequate word to describe *Iguassu Falls*! Imagine, if you can, 5 or 6 Niagara Falls lined up next to one another with some forested gaps between. Then, imagine being so close to some of the raging water that you can almost touch it; getting drenched from the mists and often being in the middle of a rainbow. Only then can you begin to imagine its enormity, power, and serenity, amidst u hydraulic chaos! And, to boot, you are in the middle of a tropical rain forest, replete with lizards, little monkeys, as well as great varieties of birds and delicately-colored butterflies, where playful little Coatimundi's play at your feet, looking for a handout.

IGUASSU FALLS- A VERY SMALL PORTION

We visited the Brazilian side of the Falls the next morning, and were dazzled by our first look at the panorama. For over two miles along the sides of the two confluent rivers, the *Iguassu* and the *Parana*, over 250 falls spill over the cliffs, some from a height of over two hundred feet. An unbelievable amount of water flows downstream; reddish tinged in places as it goes over the falls. About 12 miles upstream on the Rio Parana is the gigantic *Itaipu Dam*, reputedly the world's largest hydroelectric facility, operated jointly by Brazil and Paraguay. We walked about a mile along an ever descending walkway, aghast at the incredible scene, until we reached the largest falls, called *Garganta del Diablo* (Devil's Throat) - and were here overpowered by the noise and mist. We were told that this side offered a better panoramic view of the entire Falls system, while the Argentinian side, that we were to visit tomorrow, really gets you up close and personal. Fortunately, a 50 cent up-elevator ride got us back to street level. Tired, but immensely impressed, we were left off at the *Foz* for a very late lunch and a hunt for an elusive international ATM machine to replenish the Newbrough's *Real* supply. We ran into this difficulty at all our stops - but there were plenty of national ATMs (*Bancomats*). Likewise, there was no such problem for e-mail stations, which were in some cases located in hotels. Exhausted, we barely made it back to the safety of the hotel pool and, later, the restaurant - a hard day!

The next morning we checked out of our hotel, loaded our stuff in the van, and drove off to see the Argentinian side of the Falls. Crossing the border (both ways, for we were to fly to Rio later in the afternoon from the Brazilian-side airport) was made easy for *Iguassu* tourists. We were first taken to a series of walkways that took us across some of the smaller falls; at a high level, and then at a lower level, ending in a long uphill walk back to ground zero. Fortuitously, a camcorder professional took pictures of our group during the entire tour, and we purchased an English version of the tape, making up for the lack of my stolen camcorder.

We were then taken to a boat landing, *Puerto Canoas*, where about 12 of us were loaded onto a small single-outboard-powered skiff, told to put on life preservers, and headed out to a landing near the edge of the very top of the boiling *Giganta*. We didn't want to think of what could have happened if the engine conked out — it was a case of 'relax and enjoy' skirting near the edge of the cauldron, prayer beads busily at work! Once safely at the platform, we went down a long walkway that was somehow erected at the cataract's edge. The further along we went, the wetter we got. It was awesome - a climax to a fantastic two days of exploration. And so, Hi, Yi, Yi-Yi, we were off to our last stop - *Rio De Janiero*, two or so flight hours away.

We thought we had a plane change at Sao Paulo, one of the largest cities in the world, so when the plane came down in what was obviously a big city, I hustled to get our stuff off. I was on my way out, when a flight attendant pointed out that this was *Curitiba* (Who, What, Where, Why????)- a suburb local airport. We settled back, took off again, and eventually reached Rio, We landed through some evening overcast, thus being temporarily denied some wondrous sights through the airplane's windows.

We were met by a guide, who said he would be with us throughout our stay in Rio. He turned out to be a marvel! He was a native '*Carioca*' (that's a redundancy, a Carioca is a native of *Rio*), who spoke fluent English and French. He had lived in *Brussels* and *Lausanne* and had

had some schooling in *Geneva* - in Government - while living in Switzerland. He knew his city, and the songs, and appreciated our senior citizen status by not pushing us too hard. He truly made the Rio visit a pleasure and alleviated our fears about cut-throats and pickpockets. What the 'hay, I had already lost my camcorder, what more could they do to me?

On the way from the airport to our hotel, Marcelo explained the geography of Rio. It has two main ocean beach sections, *Copacabana* and *Ipanema,* which are blocked off from the downtown area by a series of hills through which traffic tunnels run. On the inland side from *Ipanema* Beach is a very large lagoon which borders on a large mountain park whose peak is *Corcovado,* the site of the magnificent statue, "*Christ of the Andes*", whose outstretched arms seem to bless the community, if not the world. On the inland side of the hills bordering *Copacabana* Beach is the large downtown area which ends at the shore of *Guanabara Bay,* which includes the harbor and yacht club. At the entrance to the bay, at the tip of *Copacabana,* is the funny looking 'Sugar *Loaf*' mountain, while the far end of the bay features a 10 mile long bridge to the town of *Niteroi,* site of a stunning (architecture-wise) Museum of Contemporary Arts. Our hotel, which we reached around 8pm, was the *DeBret;* right on Copa Beach, near the fortress that separates Copa from *Ipanema*. Our only disappointment (Gustavo, please note) was that our rooms were 'inside', not affording a beach view. We would have gladly paid a few extra shekels! But, we were too exhausted to make a move.

RIO – TRAIN TO 'CHRIST OF THE ANDES'

The next morning, Marcelo picked us up - an hour late, presumably. It turned out that during the night Rio had gone back to standard time, and we were rarin' to go an hour early! Donna took advantage by finding a nearby cyber café. We then were off on the city tour, featuring a visit to *Corcovado*. On the way to the Alpine-like train that struggles up the steep incline, we passed by the Art Museum, the big shopping mall building, the beautiful old *Candelaria* Church, and the edge of the downtown district. The train ride up the hill was very scenic. We passed several small communities seeming hanging in mid-air over 'cliffs. Once on top, we got our first view of the vista below us at a staging area, prior to beginning the grueling 220-step climb to the base of the 40-50 foot high statue of Christ. From here the view was even more impressive - the whole city lay before us! This, along with *Iguassu*, was clearly one of the high points of the trip!

On the way back to the hotel, Marcelo pointed out the usual Sunday flea ("Hippie") market in *Ipanema*, and suggested that we lunch at a favorite restaurant at the edge of the market, and to look for a special pre-Carnivale parade that would start there around 4pm. After a while, we gathered ourselves together and taxied back to the flea market plaza and found the *Casa da Feijoada* (Fayz-jo-ada), which features a traditional Brazilian - spread including black beans and rice and various pieces of pork and beef. Historically, this was a poor man's left-over stew concoction, but it turned out so good (as, indeed it was, in SPADES!) that we vowed to return and to have our last meal there late afternoon Wednesday prior to going to the airport. Fully sated, the others somehow managed to look over the flea market and made several key purchases. I would have none of it, and instead looked in vain for an international ATM. We had agreed during the morning to have Marcelo add - at $50 per head - a tour of Sugar Loaf and downtown Rio, and I needed some cash to pay our share.

We then made an excursion to see the doll babies on *Ipanema* Beach and looked for the parade. Not finding it, we went back to the hotel with the intention of hitting the beach. The temperature was a nice 88 to 92 degrees during our stay. On arrival at our hotel, we found a huge brou-ha-ha going on at the beach just opposite our hotel. This turned out to be the parade we were looking for! There were thousands of people in the troupe, some costumed, some bare-breasted or bottomed, most slowly shuffling, samba-like, accompanied by highly amplified samba music and pulsating jungle drums; moving at a snail's pace down the beach. We decided to watch from the comfort of the Hotel's bar, which overlooked the beach. When finally the 'marchers' moved down the beach a way, Don and I hit the sand and water, and got an up-close look at the procession on our way back to the hotel. Like the parade in *Montevideo*, we felt we getting some of the atmosphere of the real Carnivale.

The next morning, with a new guide and a large 'multilingual' bus, we were taken on an hour's ride to the small port of *Itacuruca*, whence we boarded a small (motor-driven, no sails) schooner for a day at a tropical island, *Ilha* (i.e., isle) *do Bernardo* in lovely *Sepitiba* Bay (many summer vacation homes were seen on the several islands and the peninsula on the way. To soften us up during the half hour voyage, with a stop off-shore for swimming from the boat, we were plied with a choice of the two native aperitifs: *Batida*, a sugar cane liquor (something like rum) based drink, with mixed juices, mangos, passion fruit, coconut, papaya and lime; and *Cazpirinha*: limes crushed with sugar and the sugar cane liquor, '*Cachaca*'. We had faced the same choice as part of the previous feijoada spread, and again I choose the *Batida*; the other being too sour for my taste. It is reputed that a few of either will easily see you though the day!

The island was indeed a tropical one. Before the sumptuous lunch we hit the beach and swam in the lagoon-like waters. After lunch, those who could joined a bunch of musicians and dancers and samba'd away the afternoon. Don joined in the fun, and in a memorable moment, played 'bull' to a exuberant Spanish visitor's toreador. Donna fortunately documented the event with her camera. Following the loss of my camcorder, she had been assigned camera-person duties. She produced over two hundred photos, most of which were put in the scrap book that Pat assiduously composed, and which you will be forced, kicking and screaming, to browse over when you visit us.

Others went back to the beach until the warning bell rang. Pat and I were too stuffed to do anything but watch. We boarded the schooner for the return, and as we pulled away from the dock, all the island personnel came to wave us 'aloha'. The band and dancers returned to the port on our boat - so the beat went on. It was a fun day - a respite from the grim business of sight-seeing.

As noted before, we had added the *Sugar Loaf* trip to our agenda, and while we found the view again gorgeous, it was somewhat redundant to the one from *Corcovado*. This is probably why Gustavo did not schedule it, although it is a ritual for a visit to Rio. More interesting was the ride up to the peak. It was necessary to take two separate, very crowded, gondola systems to get there. Moreover, airplanes headed to the airport routinely flew a bit out of their way to show *Sugar Loaf* to their passengers. This led to visions of the fabled Italian gondola tragedy as we were suspended in mid-air.

This day's tour ended by a visit to downtown Rio - a large area with many skyscrapers. We saw two great sites: the City Cathedral is the most unusual church we have ever seen! It must be 300 feet at the base of the conical structure. The slanting sides have vertical slits of stained glass figures. The building is golden in color. The insides include a huge viewing area, plus a separate more informal large chapel, along with the usual appurtenances that you see in all churches, but here enhanced by two striking large white marble wall-inset murals. The courtyard contained a very tall conical steel tower structure, the top of which held a large cross.

RIO- DOWNTOWN – NEW CATHEDRAL SAN SEBASTIAN

Marcelo then took us to the dedicated street and staging area where the Carnivale takes place. By plan, we were scheduled to depart two days before it began. The showplace is a wide (50-60 feet?) street about a half mile long surrounded on each side by football field-like stands. Each Samba Club (the equivalent of the 'Krewes' at Mardi Gras in New Orleans) has about 90 minutes to traverse the course, with individual judges being secretly placed in the viewing stands along the way. We got a look at some of the gaudy costumes during our stay. One was in our hotel lobby on a human-like frame. It cost $2000 US. We saw others, similarly priced, in stores throughout the city. We regretted our decision not to be there, but it probably was a good one - at our age. The Carnivale occurs on two night of parading and lasts all night! For the same reason, we decided against a night at a Samba night club that Marcelo offered us, especially in view of our previous tango club night in *BA*. Ah, to be young again!

In the afternoon, while the Newbrough's napped, Pat and I hit the beach for a pleasant sojourn. As Don and I had noted earlier, the water is 'dirty' - people leave all sorts of trash on the beach that the water gets to before the clean-up people do. But it is wonderfully warm and has no seaweed, and is heavily subscribed to at all hours of the day. We then retired to the hotel bar, where we were entertained by a guitarist with a great voice - but heard no familiar songs that we might have forgotten. We took our last evening meal at a neighborhood bistro, where Pat, who thought she had ordered a dish with her favorite black beans and rice, instead got what she described as a 'disaster'.

On Wednesday, our last day in SA, I took an early morning walk to the fortress peninsula that separates *Copacabana* from *Ipanema*, stopping on the way to watch - in amazement - a 4-man beach volley ball game in which only feet, head, and chest were engaged! Don and I then did the beach for a last swim. Finally, we each bought a coconut at a Beach-side kiosk; sipped half and brought them back for the ladies to try. They were only so-so. We finished packing and left our bags in hotel storage as we checked out. We happily 'killed' the afternoon (Marcelo was to pick us up to take us to the airport at 5pm) by putting in some bar time, where we collaborated on recalling the high points of the trip to help write this journal, and then went back to the *Casa da Feijoada* for late lunch. At the airport, after showing our appreciation to Marcelo, we were unbelievably hit with a $37 per 'departure' tax (this after paying the $60 per for a visa!). Even the tax collector admitted it a gigantic rip-off. Don't buy Brazilian beef!!!

The long flight back to Chicago was uneventful, aided by good food and a good movie and the marvelous sleeping pill. On the other hand, the Chicago-LA leg seemed to last forever, not at all helped by continuous 100 mph head winds. We arrived home at noon to 60 degree overcast weather, and remembered that it had been 92 on *Copacabana* only yesterday; but think of the Newbrough's temperature shock of an 80 degree drop! Aside from that (i.e., the camcorder loss and the 2 pounds which I gained), Mrs. Lincoln, it was a great, thoroughly enjoyable trip. I hope you enjoy reading it as much we did; those of you foolhardy enough to have read THE WHOLE THING!

Chapter 10

BOATING ON THE BALTIC - 2002

For years, we've wanted to see St Petersburg, and especially the Hermitage. We had visited Russia - Moscow and Baku, in 1973; generally liked what we saw; and desired another return to my 'roots'. After all, my father was born near Kiev. He, the youngest of 8 brothers and 3 sisters, came over at age 10; first to Toronto and thence to Philadelphia, in the late 1890's. Thus his memory of the 'Old Country' was practically nil. The glories of the *Hermitage* were storied: We had to see it in person! Coupled with this cultural anticipation, was our desire to visit Copenhagen to see how Nancy, the widow of my recently departed Navy buddy, Tommy Carrig, was getting along. Here's how it happened:

In January, 2002, we started to organize yet another of our 'last trips' with our then favorite travelling companions, Don and Donna Newbrough of Ames, Iowa - who had been with us on previous explorations in Israel/Egypt, a Mexican Riviera cruise, and last year's land jaunt in South America. We found a travel agency specializing in Baltic Sea cruises. They came up with two possibilities for a late July embarkation, both featuring the two days we wanted in St. Pete's and ending in Denmark. The longer one included stops in Germany and several Norwegian fjord town visits. We nixed it on the basis of a friend's experience from a just-completed spring cruise, "You've seen one fjord, you've seen 'em all".

We selected a cruise on the Orient Lines ship, the *MARCO POLO*, a medium size (750 passengers) liner. The sea cruise portion of the itinerary departed from Stockholm on the evening of July 25, after we had enjoyed two full sightseeing days berthed and fed aboard the ship. The next morning we were in *Helsinki* for a full day; and the following morning we arrived in *St. Petersburg* for two full days. Another overnight sail took as to *Talinn*, the capital of Estonia, for a full day's visit; whence we left for *Copenhagen*. This final leg, about 899 miles, required two nights and a day at sea; arriving in Denmark on the morning of July 31.

It luckily turned out that we had selected just the right time for the journey - the WEATHER was near perfect! The temperature was in the mid -'70's. It rained one day when we were in Copenhagen; otherwise glorious sun! We were told that *St. Petersburg* has only 32 sunlit days a year - and we hit two of them! Hallelujah! Interestingly enough, all four of the northernmost cities we visited are located at about the same north latitude figure, ~ 66 degrees, which is around 7 degrees short of the Arctic Circle. During the trip, it typically got darkish around 1l p.m. and the sun brightened things up around 4 a.m. Not quite the 'Land of the Midnight Sun'.

The cruise's fare included two 'free' nights at the Copenhagen Radisson *SAS* Scandanavia Hotel at the end of the cruise. We arranged to stay there an additional three nights to visit more with Nancy C, who lived within walking distance; and with our friends, Gudrnn and Yochen Damm from Aachen, Germany, who would join us at the hotel for a long weekend; and to see a high school mate, Ed Swanson, who lived in nearby Malmo, Sweden. I had embarked on the trip with some trepidation about my walking ability during shore excursions. I needed another operation on my spine, but could not get it done soon enough before the 'dyed in concrete - no refunds' July 23 trip departure date. Fortunately, it turned out that the medicine I was taking allowed me fairly good mobility, although I did have to sit and rest a bit whenever the pain got too bad.

Aboard the ship, we had adjoining roomy windowed cabins on the Main deck at the very aft end, affording a wonderful almost 180 degree rearward view. In many ways, a relatively 'small' cruise liner has intrinsic advantages; the chief ones being shorter food lines and an 'uncrowded' feeling. Ship's crew was composed entirely of very pleasant and competent Philippinos, except for the most-part Swedish, officer corps. All accommodations were well up to par; the food was plentiful and excellent; the entertainment varied and enjoyable, and the shore excursions we took, although expensive, were top notch. In short, don't hesitate to sail on the *Marco Polo*! It turned out that we also had selected travel in a part of the world where the least of our difficulties would be with language problems. It almost appeared as if our mother tongue was the FIRST language of the region - at least with the people who dealt with tourists.

We arrived refreshed in Stockholm on the morning of July 24 via *Continental* to Newark and *SAS* to Sweden, having had a good night's sleep thanks to sleeping pills. The Orient Line passengers were corralled at the airport and taken by bus to a downtown *SAS* hotel, where we were royally fed and assigned times to catch a bus to the ship. With a couple of hours to 'kill', we took a walk and visited the capital city's (and Sweden's) largest department store, *Ahlens City*. The Swede's have excellent designs of furniture and kitchen equipment, and these were on display. The prices were about the same as at home – no bargains apparent. We walked around the hotel area, had a drink, and were taken to the ship. Our suitcases arrived about the same time as we did and we settled down to enjoy the ship's routine which, for this cocktail hour, included a jazz hand playing by the pool.

I had been to Stockholm in the late 60's when I visited the famous Karolinska Institute, a research laboratory whom I was trying to interest in my Company's automated medical slide (blood samples) venereal disease analysis and testing machine. But that was a business trip and I didn't get to see much of the city; and Patti had not come with me; so all sights were essentially first-time ones. The next morning, we went on a half day tour and got a 'drive-by' look at the important sites: City Hall, the Royal Palace, the impressive Concert Hall, the national Museum, the Opera House, the Parliament buildings, and the quaint 'Old Town' section. The city is composed of a large number of islands of varying sizes, and consequently has a large waterfront and many bridges and canals. We purchased a souvenir guide book that nicely covers all these beauties.

We were impressed by the neatness of the city and the generally calm atmosphere. The edifices were typically European and very pleasant to look at. The main feature of the tour was a long stop at the *VASA* museum, a site devoted to showing the completely recovered (from a disastrous sinking on its maiden voyage in 1628) large 'battleship' that was meant to be the pride of the Swedish Navy. The *VASA* was over 216 feet long and displaced 1210 tons. It had 64 cannons, which no doubt contributed to the top-heaviness that did it in. It was salvaged in 1961 in wonderful shape, and is cleverly displayed in a multi-story building built around it so that each deck may be seen in some detail. We purchased an illustrated booklet that describes its history. We returned to ship in time for lunch, followed by the mandatory 'man your stations' lifeboat drill. That did it for Stockholm. We had just missed a big jazz festival, but noted that there are many jazz venues in the city, a few playing Dixieland.

The next day, we 'did' *Helsinki* -- the very nice, "everything's up to date in Kansas City" appearing capital of Finland. Here, we and the Newbrough's eschewed the 'canned' and expensive ship-planned shore excursion and reverted to our old trick of finding a roomy cab, driven by a driver who spoke excellent English. This way, we could beat the buses to the crowded places and had more choices. Our driver/guide's name was Thomas, except he spelled it with a few extra vowels and consonants. We negotiated a fixed hourly rate. He proved to be very informative and entertaining, and knew his city. He was the first of several natives we met who spoke excellent English and who, surprisingly, had never visited an English-speaking country! There were several outstanding attractions in the city. We first drove by the beautiful, mostly white-in-color vista-dominating multi~domed Russian-Orthodox *Uspenski* Cathedral and then visited the ancient Lutheran Cathedral, which is part of the Senate Square - the seat of the government. It turns out that Finland is mostly Lutheran in preference. The church is a lovely one; however, I fear I am getting blasé about cathedrals in my dotage, and am beginning to have the fjord-feeling about them now.

On the other hand, the Olympic Stadium, constructed for games that took place in the 50's, afforded a 10-story tower look-out perch that provided a great view of the entire city. On the way down in a small elevator, we were unable to get the door to open on the ground floor due to a misunderstanding of usage of the only two buttons in the damn thing! It shouldn't take a genius, right? Anyway, we had to use the squawk box to he rescued and I was forthwith no longer allowed to operate elevators during the rest of the trip.

We next proceeded to the park devoted to Finland's most famous composer - Jan Sibelius. His memorial was a massive steel structure monument constructed on the face of a rock outcropping in the form of a huge pipe organ. Standing musicians, mostly horns and clarinets, played his music. It is a lovely, serene spot - a fitting tribute to the man. Our last cab visit was to an unusual church that had been 'carved' right out of another bedrock outcropping. Naturally, it is referred to as the "Rock Church". The rotunda, capping the church area, is like a huge lid to a cooking pot. The "roof" is part wood beams and mostly glass. It is a synergistic combination of the old and the ultra modem - quite the best church design we've seen since the great cathedral in Rio and then some.

We abandoned the cab at the overcrowded waterfront market place where, amidst a great bustle of activity, we had lunch. Around us were stalls vending all types of do-dads, mixed with food stands. We were particularly impressed with the great looks of the fruits and vegetables and berries that were on sale. A multitude of tourist boats moved in and out on harbor cruises. It felt like half the town was there, though I suspect many were sightseers like us. In retrospect, *Helsinki*, along with *Tallinn* which we shall discuss later, is a gem of a city! It is clean, nicely laid out, not overcrowded (population about 500,966) and happy. A good stop!

The raison d'etre of the trip, of course, was the visit to *St. Petersburg* and the *Hermitage*. We were overwhelmed by the latter and, except for the well maintained and gorgeous palaces and the vista along the river *Neva*, underwhelmed by the former. Russia requires a VISA if you want to venture out on your own. Its cost is about $100 per person. We were also pre-warned that it might he risky to wander out on your own for fear of pickpockets and gangsters. For these reasons, we elected to take the ship's planned excursions which, although expensive (all day tour, including lunch, $175.00 per!) had the attribute of safety in numbers. In retrospect, even though we saw no real hooligan problems, I think we would have made the same choice, especially given the 'chanciness' of getting a good cab driver/guide and working our own way through the crowded museums and palaces. Alas, because of similar VISA restrictions, we were not able to meet up with distant Philadelphia cousin Matt Garfield, who by happenstance was a tourist on a canal boat which had emanated from Moscow and which had arrived in St. Pete's the same day as we.

On our first day in port, we took a long get-acquainted half day tour which provided a panoramic look at the main city sights. As we rode on the bus from she dock to city center on this Saturday, we immediately noticed two things: The amazing lack of town's people - apparently Saturday is a day of rest - and the absolute dinginess of all the buildings, including those on the wide but strictly unspectacular main drag, *Nevsky Prospekt.* Everything in sight cried for a fresh coat of paint! The streets were clean, but drab, drab, drab! The many canals we passed were also quite ordinary - nothing special like the wonderfully colorful ones we would later see in *Copenhagen* and had seen in *Amsterdam*, say, in the past. It was sad to see a city, which we later found had so much magnificence, so down on its heels.

Only when we got a view of the *Neva* river waterfront did the true ancient beauty of the city become apparent. The panorama of a vast connected phalanx of buildings lining both sides of the river bank is quite impressive. On closer inspection, however, it was apparent that many of these buildings, which had been mansions and palaces, also lacked artistic maintenance. The solid wall of buildings included shabby dwellings right next to a palace. The tourist sites, on the other hand, were wonderfully maintained inside and out. Tourism is obviously a big factor in the city's life. We learned that during the 'season', over three hundred cruise liners make essentially the same stops as we did. This averages to ~3-5 ships per day and, for St. Petersburg, doesn't include arrivals from canal boats that come up from Moscow and by other means of transportation from several locations in and out of Russia.

The half-day tour drove us by and to the main attractions: A walk through the old walled *Peter and Paul Fortress* that encloses a thin tall-spired cathedral which is the burial site of all Tsars since Peter the Great; another walk through the grounds of the lovely, soft blue pastel, and white, *Smolny* cathedral and convent; the ornate *Church of the Spilled Blood* - a close rival in splendor to the more noted *St. Basil's* by Kremlin Square - with its multi-colored, multi-surface unique Russian bulbous domes. A large busy tourist trap shopping area is across the street, replete with English-speaking salespersons and hustlers.

We were then bused to the splendid old battleship, the *Aurora*, which had signaled the start of the revolution. It was moored on the *Neva* by the Naval Parade Grounds and the large spired Admiralty headquarters. Luckily we arrived in time to see a marching band dress rehearsal for the grand NAVY DAY celebration planned for the next day. We passed, both on bus and on river boat, the well-maintained Winter Palace, which houses part of the *Hermitage* collection, and spent same time in St. Isaac's Square. On its borders are the impressive massive gold-gilded-domed *St. Isaacs Cathedral* and next door, St. Pete's swankiest hotel, where many dignitaries have stayed. There was much boating action – both tourist and commercial - on the Neva. We enjoyed a short river ride that provided a close-up view of the many buildings along the great river.

Our last day in St. Petersburg's was a rigorous sight-seeing one. The morning tour was devoted to a short two and a half hour tour of the *Hermitage* and the huge square by its side. I say 'short', because the museum is huge – larger than the *Louvre*, for example. We only covered a selected few of the old masters and impressionists. What can you say about the *Hermitage* that does it justice? It is simply overwhelming! The building itself, maintained as if it had been painted cleaned yesterday, was gorgeous - one vast room after another. Bright red colors, intricate drapes and tapestries, and golden pillars leading to outstanding painted ceilings, dominated. Where most great art museums exhibit 6 or 7 Rembrandts, the *Hermitage* has 22! And it goes on and on like that. A fortune of the world's great art treasures under one roof! I suspect the rooms devoted to Picasso have more of his work than the Picasso villa in Paris. Besides the art work, the décor and relics in the many palace rooms are equally magnificent. No doubt, this visit was the high point of our journey and the reason why all who can should make the pilgrimage. It would probably take a week to see all that there is to see. A veritable Mecca for arts lovers!

We were reluctantly hauled to an 'authentic' downtown cafe/restaurant, *Metropole*, for lunch. The word, restaurant, reads like 'pectopah' in Russian. On our earlier trip to Moscow, we wondered why so many streets seemed to be named 'Pectopah' - it took a while for the meaning to set in. This time we could relay our knowledge. The large, two story cafe was obviously set up to entertain and feed several busloads of tourists or to handle weddings or other such galas. It was semi-ornate, but nowhere near as colorful as the bright and gaudy Winter Palace. We were fed well - but on speaker-circuit chicken - albeit livened up by a touch of 'Wodka' (first one 'on the house'). The entertainment was Russian folklorico -- singers and dancers and musicians - quite nice, with brightly clad, good looking players.

Our last stop, the *Peterhof* Palace and Gardens, 20 miles outside of the city on the edge of the Gulf of Finland, was the summer palace of Peter the Great. It was almost completely destroyed by the Nazis in WW2, but has been painstakingly restored - down to the last door knob, it appears, to its original glory. And, what a glory it must have been! Like the *Hermitage*, bedecked in bright reds and blues, with much gold present in the pillars and ceilings, it's really 'fit for a Tsar' And, as in our *Hermitage* tour, we all had to put on 'booties' over our shoes to protect the floors.

The surrounding terraces and gardens feature waterfalls, canals, and a long moat down to the sea. A nice touch was the presence of a regally attired "Royal Couple" on the main terrace who would pose with you for a photo op. The 'Queen' was breathtakingly beautiful and I wanted to take her home to Mother! They say that *St. Petersburg* is pretty miserable in the winter. The harbor is iced up, unlike *Helsinki*'s, *Tallinn's*, and *Stockholm*'s year-round, ice-breaker-supported harbors So, we had arrived there at the best of times and the magnificence of the *Hermitage* and the *Peterhof* more than made up for the banality of the inner city. Tired after a very hard day, we repaired to the ship to get ready for tomorrow's adventure in Estonia.

Tallinn, the capital city of Estonia is a major Baltic port and has a population, like *Helsinki,* of about half a million. We spent a full day there and again secured the services of an SUV cab with another nice, knowledgeable driver and beat the tour buses to the viewing highlights. The town is divided into the old original walled city and a prosaic semi-modern downtown/business district and environs. Inside the walls of the old city, a large hilly area includes the noteworthy viewing areas next to an old castle, and quaint shops, churches and parliament buildings. From the hilltop, we could see the encompassing walls and the lowland modern city on one side and the farmland and the sea on the other. The ladies found a shop which featured beautiful sweaters –dutifully purchased; while the men folk observed the Estonian girls. Like their Scandanavian compatriots, they were mostly, blonde, leggy, and very comely. A wonderful country!

Even though there are no truly outstanding sites to see in Tallinn, the idea of overlooking an essentially medieval city, with cobblestone streets, guard and watch towers, red roof tiles and all, was enchanting. You were easily carried back 4000 or more years. Of particular note is Parliament Square, abutted by the Russian Orthodox *Alexander Nevsky* cathedral, with its many icons, and the colorful building that is the seat of the government. In nearby *Kadriorg* Park stands a former summer palace of Peter the Great and its well-kept gardens. The palace is now a museum, and is a stunning red and white structure. The prime minister's personal residence is adjacent to the palace.

Before returning to the ship, we asked our driver to leave us at the foot of a very busy shopping street and pick us up in a couple of hours. The ladies then commenced a massive shopping expedition, while Don and I, accompanied by glasses of beer, sat in a roadside booth and engaged in the national past-time. Our eyes were well rewarded. We then settled in for dinner and the evening's entertainment on our way to the final port-of-call - *Copenhagen* — two nights and a day-at-sea away.

We had been to Copenhagen before. I had the occasion to go to Kiruna, a city above the Arctic Circle in Sweden, on business. It has a research rocket base from which my company launched sounding rockets to observe the Aurora

Borealis. We decided to visit Tommy and Nancy in their new home outside of Copenhagen before I continued northward into the arctic cold of late September. Nancy, then a fashion illustrator, now an animated movie artist, and Tommy - sort of retired - had just moved there. Tommy's job was to run Nancy's daily drawing output in to the newspaper office for approval. I only remembered the cold, and the frantic search for a bathroom while we walked around downtown. Thus, we looked forward to this trip's more leisurely excursion at a much better, weather-wise- time of the year.

The five days we spent in *Copenhagen* were delightful! It is such a pleasant city - friendly people with a leisurely lifestyle - and we were surrounded by old friends. We disembarked from the ship, having left our luggage outside our cabin the previous night, and were immediately whisked away on a half day tour of the city. This permitted our luggage to be sent to our hotel, where indeed we did find it when we finished the morning tour. The city of a million and a half people is fairly compact, and English is spoken as a second, or first, language. The first stop on our tour was the obligatory 'Little Mermaid', right next to a small boat harbor berthing about 50 ships, mostly sail boats- which made me feel at home right away. She was smaller than I had expected and comes with a heart-wrenching story of unrequited love - which is what got her in her present 300 year 'fix'. I will not relate the story - do your own research on *Ariel*. She does present a great photo-op, however, and is always fully restored and 'aged' after vandals besmirch her.

The bus tour made two main stops after the Mermaid; the first being a visit to the *Christianborg Palace* which includes the buildings from which the government is run. The main purpose of this palace is for the Queen to use when receiving foreign dignitaries and for affairs of state.

The reception rooms had a regal feeling and were nicely decorated - not as ornate as the *Hermitage* and *Petershof*, but first rate nevertheless. Nearby, is the Town Hall square, replete with statues and a famous mechanical clock located in its tower.

The final tour stop was on the waterway front near the large square, *Amelienborg*, around which four near-identical French-style palaces are located; one for the Queen, a second, connected by an overhead walkway through an arch, for the Queen-mother; a third for the Crown Prince; and the last for visiting royalty. By luck or design, we arrived in time to witness the changing of the guard -- a cadre of troops in high furred headgear marching in precision. At both this and the earlier stop, my troubled right leg got its first real work out since the semi-successful 'road tests' in St. Pete.'s. This time, I seemed to be much improved, although still requiring some short rest stops. Fortunately, this 'better' situation prevailed throughout the rest of the stay and, indeed up to my August 26 operation. Now, in mid-September, my post- op condition was, alas, about the same as pre-op.

During the ride portion of the morning tour, we passed the major sites of the city, most of which, we would subsequently re-visit by foot or canal boat in the next few days. The most beckoning of such landmarks was the colorful *Nyhavn* (New Haven) waterfront area. This is the epitome of such fabled waterfronts throughout Europe. Its raffish buildings, all bars or restaurants on the lower floor, are multi-colored and have a block-long rows of tables and chairs for beer drinking and eating in front of them on one side. Old ships are moored alongside the quay - some obviously there permanently, trapped by low bridges through which only the low floating canal boats, filled with sightseers ducking their heads as they go under, can pass.

This area marks the start of the main concourse of several very long walk-only shopping, etc., streets which traverse the city. On the way around the city, we saw the entrance to Tivoli Gardens, the famous amusement park where we were destined to spend two evenings; the kitschy stock market building with its roof diorama of twisted snakes; the *Rosenberg Palace*, the old royal home and present displayer of the crown jewels and other artifacts and crypts; the art museum; the resplendent opera house; and the national mint. We finally arrived at our hotel, which we knew would be strategically located near Nancy's and the Tivoli Gardens on the far bank of the major waterway by which the *Marco Polo* entered the harbor. It was around 1 p.m., and we were starved. By the time we had finished lunch in the hotel, our luggage had arrived and we could move into our rooms, unpack and settle down. We called Nancy and asked her to meet us at the hotel later in the afternoon for our reunion.

We spent the evening at Tivoli Gardens, starting out with drinking beer on a warm evening while watching some remarkable acrobats performing on the main outdoor stage. Tivoli is a wondrous place –a Turkish delight for kids because of the many types of 'rides' - but equally appealing for grown-ups because of the restaurants, the entertainment, and also, the adult rides. We were amazed at the large number of people there on a week night, but Nancy explained that it is THE place for families to have a blow-out. During the last three weeks of July -we had just missed it - the annual Copenhagen Jazz Festival took place and a main venue was at the large *Tivoli Glass Theater* concert hall. We walked around the large park and settled in for dinner at one of Tommy's favorite restaurants, the *Groften*. Here I tried a delicious local dish, an Irish stew-like platter, whose name I think is '*skipper lahskovs*'.

The next morning we walked over to Nancy's and enjoyed her large many-roomed flat where they brought up their children. She showed us a painting she had done of Tommy which exactly caught the 'devil in his eye' when he worked a 'gotcha!' on you. We then started off on a long walk around the town, first ducking into the main art museum down the street from Nancy's toward Tivoli's front entrance. Now, walking parallel to the waterway, we grabbed a non-guided 'green line' canal boat at nearby Gammel Strand. These boats carry around 50 passengers and are on 20 minute centers, so you can get off at a stop, wander around, and pick up the next one. The round trip takes about an hour and a half and the fare is reasonable. However, I should point out that of all the cities we visited, *Copenhagen* had the highest prices, although nothing was outrageous.

The waterbuses are a wonderful way to see the city. Our boat proceeded past the Mint and stock exchange and into quaint *Nyhavn* district, where we were able to score a beer from a vendor who came aboard during the stop. We then proceeded across the channel past some new developments, both business and housing, and thence re-crossed the channel to arrive at the Mermaid stop. From there, we stopped on the quay where our ship was berthed and took a side trip to a fortress island in the middle of the channel, which in the old days was the 'guardian' of the harbor. On return, we stopped at the *Amalienborg* stop, noting nearby the fancy mooring dock for the Queen's vessel. The final legs had us again crossing the channel to go through the very picturesque canal in a section called *Christianhavn*, and again crossing to a stop at the lovely main library building before re-entering the canal that took us hack to Gammel Strand, just past the Tivoli stop.

Disembarking, we headed for the main walk street thoroughfare which commenced at the square abutting *Nyhavn*. We ran through a large department store, passed multitudes of specialty shops, fast food places, confectionaries - all anyone's heart could desire! Nancy found the restaurant that she liked in the Post Office and we had late lunch in a very lovely setting. The restaurant is perched on the top of the postal work area and affords a great view of the busy streets below. After lunch, we did more sightseeing and taxied back to the hotel, very tired. That evening, Nancy came by and took us to another of their favorite restaurants, down the street away from Tivoli near the banks of the large lake across the street from our hotel. We ate al fresco - watching the beautiful swans that guarded the lake. I tried a delicious Danish dish that was somewhere between steak tartare and meat loaf.

The next day, Friday, was hectic. The Newbroughs were headed back home in mid-afternoon; our friends from Aachen, Yochen and Gudrun Damm were expected at some unknown time in the afternoon, and I had arranged to see my high school classmate, Ed Swanson, for lunch. The problem was that Ed lived in *Malmo*, Sweden, a half hour train ride across the new bridge which spans the strait that separates Denmark from Sweden. On our way into port, we had passed under this bridge, with quite a hit of clearance actually, after we were sure that it would wipe out the upper superstructure of the good ship *Marco Polo*. The bridge is long and carries both cars and trains. It starts with an underground portion right after the airport and then rises majestically up towards its suspension span. Ed wanted Patti to come with me, but she had to wait far the arrival of the Damns.

The circumstances of this meeting, which we had prearranged by letter and phone before our departure from California, are unusual. Ed and I were both victims of the September 11 tragedy. We both were on our way to Philadelphia to attend our 6Oth high school reunion on September 12. Ed was in Orlando, visiting his son, and the airlines did not fly. I was near Worcester, Mass. visiting our youngest son and boarded the train to Philly at 8:30 a.m. on the fateful day. I was dumped off at New Haven and had to he rescued by my son's car. But now we had a chance for a mini-reunion. The Copenhagen train station is near Nancy's on the 'back' side of Tivoli. The train ride was pleasant and Ed was at the *Malmo* station to greet me - looking pretty much as I remembered him from our 50th reunion.

Ed then showed me around the downtown area, which had large squares and clean wide streets. To tell the truth, it looked more like an American mid-west city than a European one. Ed and his family owned a large building downtown where he conducted his business, which mostly consisted of the sale and repair of Rolex's and other high fashion watches; a trade he learned in Philadelphia after graduation. We then drove to his home in the suburbs and met his wife, Ingrid. Ed had met her after graduation, when he was treated to a trip to his 'Old Country' as a graduation present. They have a nice house which they love. We had a beer or two in the back yard and reminisced and caught up, and then had a traditional, I suspect, Swedish lunch of wonderful salmon, salad and bread. Very pleased with our short get-together, we vowed to make it to our being-planned 65th, and I got the 3 o'clock train back to the Hotel.

When I arrived, the Damns were there; and the Newbroughs, after meeting them, had departed far the airport. We first met Gudrun in 1981, when she was a law school student in Neu Isenberg, a small town near the Frankfurt airport where she grew up; and where Patti's cousin Lee lived. Gudrun and her family were celebrating her and her twin sister's birthday at a restaurant, the *Apfelwein*, that Lee had steered us to. They invited us to sit at the end of their long table, since the restaurant was jammed. I sat next to Gudrnn and we conversed in French, since at that time mein Deutsche was gestunk and her English shaky. We decided to become pen pals; she writing in English and me in German. So, we have stayed in touch while she became a Judge; married Yochen and honeymooned in California while staying with us; had two children; moved from Frankfurt environs to Aachen, Yochen's nativity city and where he was CFO of *Ericksson*'s continental office. We have had several mutual visits in between.

We spent the next two days exploring Copenhagen with the Damn's, who had never been there before. Saturday was the only day on the whole trip that the weather acted up, but we braved the rain drops and found shelter during downpours. We did the walks and waterbus rides and ate in *Nyhavn*. Gudrun and Yochen braved the adult amusement park rides in Tivoli and we ate again at *Groften*. Another delightful reunion! The Damn's left Sunday afternoon, and we spent our last evening with Nancy, and ate again at the restaurant by the lake. We returned to home on Monday afternoon, Aug 5. The next day, I started a series of tests to make sure the scheduled Friday operation would he prudent. On Wednesday, while pre-registering at the supposed operation hospital, I found that it was the wrong hospital. The August 9 operation was delayed until August 26 -- but that's another story!

Before this epic is finished, a few wards about life aboard ship: There were two outstanding events that occurred: July 29, the day we were in *Talinn*, was Patti's birthday. At dinner on-hoard that evening, as we were under weigh to Copenhagen, she got a splendiferous cake and songfest from the dining room crew to go along with the 180 carat or so diamond ring I think I gave her; The Captain's cocktail party occurred on a prior evening pre-meal ceremony. We got all duded up (I even wore a snap-on bow tie) and had a really lovely 'holding hands' picture taken. We bought out the store! Every night aboard ship there was some entertainment, and most of it was excellent. There was a permanent troop of young singers and dancers who put on great shows. We also heard twice from a very funny Irish comedian; and an excellent couple performed magic tricks; an orchestra played good music, and a very talented dance couple strutted their stuff. As I said earlier, the *Marco Polo* has much to offer and helped make this 'last' trip a wonderful one. In fact, started thinking of what our next 'last trip' would he.

Chapter 11

SOUTH-CENTRAL AMERICAN CRUISE -2004

Our Central/South American cruising adventure began with two land days in Costa Rica and ended with three land days in both *Valparaiso* and its outstanding sea side resort of *Vina del Mar* and in the Chilean capital, *Santiago*. The cruise part, aboard the Oceania Liner, *Insignia,* was relaxing, warm, and fattening. We sight-saw at each port-of-call and continued to be amazed at the tremendous influence that Spain had on the development of this part of our world. Traveling with us were our Redondo Beach friends, Morris and Jean. During the voyage, we made many other friends, who remain so to this day.

PUERTO CALDERA TO VALPARAISO
12-DAY VOYAGE ABOARD INSIGNIA
DEPARTS DECEMBER 5, 2004

DAY	PORT	ARRIVE	DEPART
Dec 5	Puerto Caldera, Costa Rica	Embark 3 pm	7 pm
Dec 6	Cruising the Pacific Ocean		
Dec 7	Fuerte Amador (Balboa), Panama	8 am	6 pm
Dec 8	Cruising the Pacific Ocean		
Dec 9	Manta, Ecuador	8 am	8 pm
Dec 10	Cruising the Pacific Ocean		
Dec 11	Salaverry, Peru	8 am	3 pm
Dec 12	Callao, Peru	8 am	8 pm
Dec 13	Cruising the Pacific Ocean		
Dec 14	Arica, Chile	8 am	4 pm
Dec 15	Cruising the Pacific Ocean		
Dec 16	Coquimbo, Chile	10 am	6 pm
Dec 17	Valparaiso, Chile	Disembark 8 am	

Except for the middle part with two stops in Peru, and the end in Chile, we had restful and congenial days at sea between the rigors of port-of-call exploring. Despite the fact that, early in the journey, we were above and below the equator with summer just beginning in South America, it was never really hot. The weather – except for one wet day at sea – was lovely. The relative coolness of this part of the world is attributed to the Humbolt current, a Gulf Stream-like flow that emanates from Antarctica.

We arrived at the San Jose airport in Costa Rico late Saturday morning and were taken to the excellent *Real Intercontinental* hotel. In the immediate future, we had the afternoon to look over the neighborhood and the next day open, prior to boarding our ship at nearby Puerto Caldera in late afternoon. We settled in and went to the lobby to seek Morris and Jean. They introduced us to new – for life – friends, Connie and Janet, who had arrived earlier from Houston.

The next day, we took a tour of the Capital – a bustling second-worldish city of over a million inhabitants. Its main attractions, none overwhelming, were the national theater, national museum, and government offices. That evening, joined by our friends who had been on the all-day rainforest tour, we ate at a converted monastery, *Grill La Cava*, located high on a hill overlooking the town. The view was spectacular and the cuisine French.

Meanwhile, while we were touring the city, our friends and traveling companions opted to take a ride through the nearby dense 'rain forest'- the *Braulio Carrilo National Park* - riding in 6-person cable cars suspended from tree tops. They pronounced it as a 'very good' tour, with lots of birds and forest animals in view. Connie later wrote about it, and I will 'use' her words: "After viewing an explanatory video, we took a short walking tour. We were warned to watch out for deadly snakes, but were assured that they had an anti-venom that was effective if you get it into your system within three hours of an attack. Alas, the station was at least a three hour drive away. Most of the animals waited for nightfall to make an appearance, but we did see a few beautiful birds and many gorgeous bright turquoise butterflies. We were then bussed to *Rio Danta* for lunch, looked around this charming town, tight against the dense forest, and returned to the hotel for dinner at the Monastery."

The following day, Sunday, we all drove through tropical settings of great beauty and spent two-plus hours plus lunch at a coffee plantation – a pleasant stop-over on the way to the port to board our ship. We were told that we would tour a coffee field and then see a show to learn about the '*Ticos*' – a nickname for Costa Ricans. A guide told us of the romance of coffee, with demonstrations of bean picking and shucking. This reprised into a clever play in a theater-like setting- again featuring the history of coffee. We had lunch in the plantation's dining room and then visited their gift store. We bought some coffee beans to take home.

Leaving the plantation on a bus carrying our luggage, we headed for our departure port, Puerto Caldera. The surrounding town was a poor one - obviously not a tourist attraction. Apparently, the good beaches are further up and down the coast. Our ship is fairly new, having been built for the now-bankrupt Renaissance line. It holds a max of 684 passengers, but we are pleased to hear that we have less than 400. We steam out of the harbor- band playing-settle in and undergo the required 'life boat' drill. We have a day at sea 'til we reach our next port-of-call.

The next stop, the port of *Balboa* (*Fuerte Amador* – a peninsula that juts out from *Balboa*) that serves Panama City, provided a historical look of the impact of the Canal and the various forces, American and French, which shaped the modern city. There were a number of sight-seeing attractions offered: dugout rides through the jungle to meet the *Embera* tribe; a tour of Gatun Lake; an aerial tram; and the City tour. Janet and Connie and the rest of our group signed up for the 3-hour sky dome train tour along the Canal, while we chose the City tour. We were bused from the harbor to the entrance to the new city where the Norte Americanos have set up shop, and where much high class development was proceeding. The new city has many, many skyscrapers of typically 20-25 stories, which are mostly condos. We were told that they then went for less than $100,000 for 3 bedrooms. The old colonial city, pillaged by the pirate Henry Morgan, now consists of well-preserved ruins. Though Panama City is modern and mostly English speaking, and prices are very reasonable, we could see no compelling reason to live there.

We had been through the Canal on ship on two previous occasions, but it was a first for the rest of our group. They were ‘tendered’ to a bus from our ship and thence bused to the 1930s-style excursion train. They were not overly impressed with the trip. At the Caribbean side, *Puerto de Cristobal*, they had a leg-stretching break, but the truth was – they couldn't see too much from the speeding train, which pretty much paralleled the canal, but was too far inland to see lock operations. We departed – band again playing - for Ecuador around 4 pm.

After a day at sea, we arrived at *Manta*, Ecuador, whose main claim to fame is its proximity to the nearby village of *Montecristi*, the home - incongruously - of Panama hats! The temperature was a balmy 90 degrees, not surprising since we were close to the Equator. The village itself was non-descript, albeit everyone was selling hats and other goodies. The price of a *Panama* varied from $30-300. Pat bought a very colorful tapestry. In *Manta* city, we also visited a very interesting factory that makes buttons, as well as very lovely carvings of animals and palm trees. These are carved out of what they call 'vegetal ivory' (*Tagua*) nuts, which are the fruit of a wild palm that grows in the tropical forest. You would be hard put to tell the difference from tusk ivory! We then see the Rio Manta, whose water is a bright red as it empties into the ocean at *Tarqui*, a popular beach resort. Our last stop is the Central Bank Museum-which has an archeological exhibit representing the 7 cultures that existed in these environs from 4200 BC to 1530 AD.

En route to our next stop, we crossed the equator on 12/10/04 and were witness to the elaborate ceremony initiating 'Polliwogs' – those who have never previously crossed – into the secret Society of Shellbacks. Connie participated in the initiation – kissed the fish and was doused in some sticky, gooey stuff. It took her and her clothes 2 days to recover!

Two mornings after departing from Ecuador, we arrived at our first stop in Peru – *Salaverry*, the port for *Trujillo*, the second largest city, after its capital, *Lima*. Excursions offered were to Machu Picchu, Lake Titicaca or the big city. We all chose the latter; the mountain excursion being too arduous a trip for us. *Trujillo* is of interest because it was the home of successive, fairly advanced, native civilizations, and thus an archeological wonderland. Its ancient town square, *Plaza de Armas*, is picturesque with its Spanish colonial architecture, featuring a lovely church on one corner. We visited the ancient pyramid-shaped '*Temple of the Sun*' and '*Temple of the Moon*' adjacent sites. The pyramids are quite high and are made of adobe bricks. Because of the dry climate, they will probably last forever. These 'digs' are akin to the sites in Egypt, but even older! The Spaniards displaced the Incan Empire in the early 1500's. Here, for the first time, we began to grasp the tremendous changes and influence that the Spaniards brought, which forever set the path on which most of South America has trodden. The town of *Trujillo* itself was second worldish, but had a beautiful cathedral and wonderful monasteries that went on and on, replete with fine artistic works.

We also visited *Chan Chan*, a community composed of seven citadels spread over an 8 square mile area surrounded by a massive adobe wall. It was built around 1300 AD and once had a population of over 60,000. There was a lot of ancient artwork on the citadel walls. On the inside of one, there was a large artesian well and pool, which was used as their water supply. Now there were water lilies blooming and ducks swimming. Returning to the ship, we were treated to view a nice adjoining seaside village, with a band playing and many canoe-sized fishing boats made of reeds; a scene from the cover of the *Saturday Evening Post*!

Off to Callao, gateway to Lima, the Capital of Peru, and – at > 8 million population – its largest city. Our time in Lima was limited because there is not much out of the ordinary to see. We passed a big casino with a Statue of Liberty and a big flashing sign that says "New York, New York' in front of it. We zipped through the wealthy Miraflores area to be dropped off at a large market. We were allotted two hours to mingle with the hundreds of vendors housed in stalls inside buildings on both sides of the street. Then we went to the *Museo de Oro del Peru* – the gold museum. It required a small entry fee into the grounds that are marked by numerous upscale shops on both sides of the winding walkway to the museum proper. The gold museum itself consists of an upper floor and a basement. There are incredible collections of military gear, including weapons and uniforms. Gold, silver and copper once were plentiful here and it appears that the ancient civilizations adorned themselves for special occasions. There are several well-preserved Indian-looking costumes made of leather, metal and feathers. Also present are mummies, some in good condition, and massive amounts of gold objects such as cups, utensils, knives and other paraphernalia. It is all too much and we are ready to return to our ship to indulge in another bout of Trivia (Connie, Janet, Morris and I were the team).

Our next port stop was *Arica*, in very northern Chile – and gateway to the famous Atacama desert - the world's driest! There are many places where rain has never been documented and long stretches where no organic life can be found. No wonder it is now a playground for potential Lunar and Martian explorers. Arica's history is varied. It was once part of Bolivia and provided that now landlocked nation with a seaport to ship its silver production. Later, it belonged to Peru, finally turning Chilean as a result of a war. Now Chile allows tariff-free seaport access for both Peru and Bolivia.

The contrast between Chile and Peru is evident even though we are only 12 miles from the Peruvian border. *Arica* is a bustling place, watched over by a huge statue of Christ atop the mountain to the right of where we are docked. One of his arms extends to the north and the other to the south while he oversees the harbor. We walked from the dock to the town - a short distance. On the way, there was a market set up in front of a small wrought iron sanctuary. The building is distinct in that it was made of iron and pre-constructed in France and its architect was none other than Gustave Eiffel. There is a second iron building in town, also designed by Eiffel to serve as a Custom's House. It is now a museum. One of the main attractions is at the top of the '*Morro de Arica*' – a very high hill accessible by an arduous walking climb. At the end of the line, there was an old fortress and a museum that contained arms from the war of liberation. We decided that it would be too difficult to make the trek, but some of our fellow travelers did. They said it was good exercise and a good view, but going back to our ship was probably the right decision for us.

Overnight, we steamed to *Coquimbo*, an important Chilean port that ships fruit grown in the nearby *Elqui Valley*. Papaya and grape plantations are scattered throughout the valley. Wines from this region are gaining an international reputation. The real local action however was in the nearby town of *La Serena*, the second oldest city of Chile and which proved to be worth exploring. It lies between the Altacama Desert and the rich agricultural central valley it seques into. Its population was ~230,000 and its historic colonial buildings were restored in the 50s. Because it was once an important missionary center, it has over 30 churches. It is also a popular weekend destination for residents of Santiago because of its many fine beaches spread along the local coastline. *Plaza de Armas*, in the center of the town, presents a multitude of shopping opportunities – to the delight of our Houstonites. The streets were flower-lined, replete with tiny little shops. But, unhappily, they found that it was necessary to convert dollars into local coin. Back at the ship, we enjoyed a wonderful 'last supper' and were royally entertained as we headed for deportation at Valparaiso the next morning.

Valparaiso is Chile's second largest city and its busiest port. It has a dramatic and beautiful port and is built on 17 hills surrounding the harbor. The harbor is in a large cove, with a long narrow peninsula going westward into the ocean. The city itself seems to be in a bowl, with a lot of housing - many Victorian- style with large porches and gingerbread trim, built into the steep hillsides, and appearing to be ready to fall into the harbor any minute. Elevator trams (ascensores) and questionable staircases make the hillsides look pretty treacherous, but the residents' view must be worth the trouble.

Many passengers remained on the ship as it continued its voyage around Cape Horn to Buenos Aires and Montevideo. A friend of Connie's had given her a section from the *Dayton Daily News* in which a travel writer described his version of that leg of the journey taken earlier: "The Pacific ocean didn't live up to its name. First, we were bucked up and down, then rolled from side to side. In my cabin, four decks above water level, the bigger waves sent water sloshing around the portholes. It was like looking into a giant front-loading washing machine set on *beserk*." On day 11 of the 14 day extension, he reported that the seas had waves topping 65 feet high and winds of more than 92 mph! Hearing this, we were glad that we had earlier decided not to sail on from Valparaiso.

We toured Valparaiso and its environs. Most interesting was the trip out the peninsula to *Vina del Mar* – a favorite beach town – the Atlantic City of western South America. We passed a luxurious casino that backed up to a narrow park with a river cutting through it headed for the sea. Lined up for tourist and those romantically inclined were a number of horse-drawn carriages. The palm tress and new high-rise condos remind us of Miami. Still, the dominating aura is European, as on the French and Italian Rivieras. It is obviously a sophisticated and affluent resort. Apparently Europeans and wealthy Chileans who had visited Europe brought back many ideas that they applied in building up *Vina del Mar*. They built mansions and castles with beautiful gardens, many of the latter now being city parks. The mansions were positioned for a panoramic view of the ocean. One of them clings to a precipitous slope; another is perched on a cliff; while a third is sitting atop a huge rock – an island in the sky hovering above the sea.

Then, after lunch, we were off to Santiago, the capital of Chile, 75 miles away at the foothill of very impressive mountains – part of the Andes. We drove through a long tunnel going through the coast mountain range and miraculously entered the middle of a valley that must be the size of California's Napa/Sonoma. To the South and North of us, as we headed inland, we saw nothing but fields of vineyards. It was an amazing, beautiful sight! We arrived in the city just prior to rush hour and settled in at our hotel, where we would spend two nights at the end of our journey. Connie and Janet were leaving later in the evening. We were sorry to part with them, and promised to keep in touch – which we have to this day.

Alas, neither of us recall much about our tour in Santiago – and, this time, Connie's writing could not come to the rescue. We recall that it was a very European-type city with large esplanades and parks. The streets were well maintained and wide. There were many fountains and much statuary. The restaurants were uniformly good. We took a city tour. The town is comfortable. We left for home feeling all is well in Chile. All in all, it was a very interesting and worth-while pleasant journey. We saw places and things we had never expected to see. What more could you ask for?

Chapter 12

DOWN THE DONAU - 2006

We had never been on a trip aboard a river cruiser, and got enthused when our Lodi, Ca. travel agent, Brenda, proposed a May/June *Uniworld*-sponsored Danube River trip from Budapest to the Black Sea. We persuaded our fellow traveler Houston friends, Connie Voss and Janet Hicklin to come along, as well as our friend Jean Dixon, wife of our recently deceased sailing crewman, Dr. Bill Dickson. Connie rounded up three Texas friends (Cam and Vicki McMartin, and KayDee Cooper) with whom we were to share the many adventures to follow. The itinerary, for us, was to fly from LA to *Prague* (via Paris), train to *Budapest*, and fly back home from *Bucharest*. At the last minute, Janet had to cancel because of illness. Pat did not keep her normal daily Journal, but Connie did – and later wrote an excellent account, which we used extensively to compose this travelogue. Make no mistake about it, Connie did the heavy lifting here. All we did was to change her present tense writing into past tense and add personal notes.

A Uniworld representative was there to meet us at the *Prague*, Czech Republic, International Airport. Shortly, the Texans also arrived and joined us for a ride to our hotel. The Ambassador hotel is centrally located in Old Town *Prague*. It is nicely Old World with high-ceilinged comfortable rooms that include a Jacuzzi, a shower, a day bed, a sitting area and an alcove fitted with two very comfortable beds. Downstairs one can sit in the bar and watch the many pedestrians stroll down the very wide and popular street called *Vaclavske namesti*. A casino, a bar/restaurant, a meditation center and a breakfast room are below street level. There are also banquet rooms and a spa/massage room.

We weary travelers met for cocktails at 6:30 PM and then enjoyed our first dinner together. We shared a succulent meal of roast duck, a thick ham slice and roast pork that all sat on a rich gravy. The meats shared the plate with two sauerkrauts (one white cabbage and another of red cabbage). We were also given several slices of the famed *Prague* dumplings. You sop the gravy with the rather bland tasting dumplings. Then, although I wanted to try the local Disco, Pat and our younger travel mates declined and we all then opted for a good night's sleep

Our group met in the morning for a luxurious breakfast. We enjoyed a bread slice which we cut in half to make a breakfast sandwich of two kinds of thinly sliced meats and a slice of cheese; along with fresh fruit and yogurt, a sausage and a *palacinka* (a crepe with jam and clotted cream). Coffee and juice rounded out the meal. Then, we were off on a city inspection.

Peter, our guide in *Prague*, greeted us at 9:00 for a half-day tour. We joined hundreds of other tourists for a taste of the city. Peter told us that our hotel is located in the heart of Wenceslas Square; which is not a square at all, it's really a rectangular shaped promenade. We walked through the courtyards of Prague Castle and a portion of the Charles Bridge (over the *Vltava* River). We had been preceded on the bridge by many famous persons: The Pope had walked across the bridge, the Queen of England also walked across the bridge, but President Bill Clinton chose to ride in a limo across the bridge; later he played his saxophone for the citizens of *Prague*. The thirty sculptures of Saints that line the bridge were being replaced with duplicates so that the originals can be placed in a museum and not left out in the damaging elements. St. John of Nepomuk is a popular statue-- touching a certain spot on his monument and making a wish at the same time is supposed to fulfill the wish. There is also a beautiful crucifix at the bridge. The bridge offers yet another great view: that of *Hradcany Castle*, which we then inspected. (Go to <davidsanger. com/stockimagaes/4-960-149.johnnepomuk> for a photo of the statue and other beautiful photos of Prague.)

Peter pointed out the ugly former Radio Free Europe building with bomb bunkers still in front (Radio Free Europe has since moved to a secret location that everyone knows). The Hilton Hotel was pointed out because Bill Clinton and his entourage had taken over the complete hotel during the Clinton visit (all 365 rooms); and it was also where Michael Jackson had stayed. Peter next showed us a yellow building with statues of great composers standing guard at its roof line (the State Opera House). We also saw St. Vitus Cathedral (part of the Castle courtyard and the home of the dear old 'St. Vitus Dance'); Charles Square; *Malostrannshe* namesti (Lesser Quarter Square); and the Dome of the St. Nicholas Church in Mala Strana.

We got a brief view, in passing, of the Jewish cemetery that is much higher than street level because they had to bury the bodies on top of one another; and an ancient Jewish Synagogue. We visited the square in front of the Astronomical clock and waited in the street for the rare clock to do its disappointing thing (figures slouching around in a circle). We took Peter's advice and went to a local restaurant for lunch. The sign showed a very fat boy with big blue pants. The tables were full upstairs, so we descended downstairs to a cave-like basement where colorful cartoons are painted on the walls (most of which were a bit off color). One cartoon showed a big-busted woman behind the steering wheel of her car. The car is on fire and she is crying for help. Four good Czech men come to her aid and pee on the car.

The food was good and plentiful. We enjoyed a "sauered entrée" of thick bacon and beef roasted to a crunchy outer texture with little fried balls of mashed potatoes on the side. We all enjoyed a large glass of the local beer. We soon learned that goulash is not just Hungarian, but is prepared in numerous ways all across Eastern Europe and is served with potatoes, rice or polenta along with white and/or red cabbage that is not sour, but is slightly sweet. Released from the rigors of the tour, we strolled, shopped and snapped pictures like good tourists are supposed to do.

Tired and relaxed, we were enjoying drinks in our hotel lobby when, amazingly, our German friend, Gudrun, ran across the room screaming and crying. She reached me and threw her arms around me and kissed me and then did the same to Pat. Soon her son, Peter, a handsome 12-year old boy, and her very pretty 17-year old daughter, Marina, and their dad (Jochen) join us. Our traveling companions, and we, all had tears in our eyes at the touching reunion. The Damm family had traveled all day by car from their home in Germany just to see us. Pat and I and the (whole) Damm family sat around and caught up with our doings in the hotel lobby and then went to a popular Czech restaurant further down the avenue. It was crowded and there were 20 or so persons in line waiting to get in the front door. We were jabbering with the Damms and failed to pay attention to some young guys pushing and shoving in the waiting line. Halfway through dinner, Patti looked for something in her purse and instead found what every tourist fears - her wallet had been pick-pocketed! We finished dinner and scavenged the neighborhood trashcans to no avail. Finally, we gave up and the Damms departed for their hotel and we to ours- where I spent the next 3 hours on the phone to the U.S. canceling credit and ATM cards. Surprisingly, the next morning - before we departed for Budapest –a messenger from England brought us a replacement set of VISA cards!

In the meantime, the rest of our companions broke up and did their own thing. Jean wanted to do some things by herself, so the remaining four decided to follow Peter's advice again and went to the *Mucipalities* for dinner. It is located in a large old building with a theater and several restaurants inside. They checked out all the restaurants and settled for one that had tall ceilings, beautiful chandeliers and looked as though it also had once been a theatre (The *Francouzska Restaurare*). Some irresistible items listed on the menu were -

Hot Creams from Sheep Cheese
Tenderloin of Pyrenees Pig
Fallow Deer Saddle Back with Juniper Berry and Rosemary
Rosily Baked Veal Meat
Hors D'Oeurves Carved

They laughed so hard that they had difficulty ordering. But the meal turned out deliciously, including the grand "treble clef" dessert--a thin chocolate cake cut into the shape of a grand piano. A chocolate ganache supported a smooth chocolate piano lid. The keyboard was of white and dark chocolate. To the side was a small pot of raspberry sauce with white/dark chocolate notes across the top. On the plate was a spun candy treble clef. Then a cognac cart appeared with a different cognac for every year since about 1920. Vicki decided to end the meal with a bit of cognac. The man asked the year of her birth. (She lied.) He said 'no', she could not possibly be that old, so she lied again and selected an even more recent year. He was satisfied with this and she enjoyed this libation to complete her dining experience, until we discovered that the sip of cognac had cost $35. Now, they all wondered what it would have cost had she been older?

While in Prague, as we were sight-seeing with the Damms, Connie and company kept busy on their own. They attended an hour-long *vivat Mozart* concert by a local chamber ensemble at the Church of St. Martin in The Wall. Included in the concert were *Canzonetta* (Don Giovanni) and *A Little Night Music* by Mozart and *Mannheim Symphony No. 3* by Stamitz. They shopped and discovered that prices were as high as they were at home, especially for antiques. Connie's hobby and part time weekly work deals in bric-a-braq. Vicki and KayDee share in this avocation. They found lots of fake Gallé glass and a lot of real Royal Dux porcelains and Mosier glass (old and new). They found that Herend porcelain, even though manufactured in nearby Hungary, was as expensive as it is in the States.

The street food smelled so delicious and looked so great that Connie and KayDee vowed to have at least one street meal before leaving. Our friends all did so, and it was reported delicious. They served them all types of tasty sausages on super breads or rolls, and they were yummy! Connie next had to return to the shop she had visited the day before and buy more hand painted plastic rings (to resell) and more wonderful gift boxes, unlike any she'd seen. KayDee and Jean each bought an amber necklace and Vicki bought a 'to-die-for' silver/amber ring and bracelet. They finally stumbled across an antiques store that had something affordable, so Connie bought several nice pieces of jewelry for about $100. One was an old sterling pin with a cutout of the *Prague* skyline

While Pat's wallet was being lifted elsewhere, Cam found an unusual restaurant for our friends' last evening in Prague called 'HOT - *Asia Meets Europe*'. The place was replete with lots of red flowers surrounding the "summer garden" that faced the promenade. Inside, there were red rose petals scattered along the countertop in the ladies' bathroom and cool chrome barstools and red upholstered chairs, as well as live entertainment in the form of a pianist. It was very chic. They could tell that it would indeed get HOT after around 10:00 PM. The fusion-style food was great, too!

So ended our adventure in *Prague*. We headed for the train station early in the morning of June 6, 2006. The van dumped us outside and we were at a total loss as to where to go to meet our train. There was no one to help us with luggage and there were no ramps in site...only multitudes of stairs. Worse yet, no one spoke enough English to help us. Finally, Cam had spotted our train to Budapest on the roster and we barely had enough time to make it. The train was clean and comfortable as we headed across the countryside through Slovakia. Lynn Campbell, a lady that goes to the same beauty shop and beautician as Connie, was on the same train along with her friend Emily! What a coincidence! They were going to join 8 other friends, all Houstonians, on our same river cruise ship in Budapest. (We would learn later that their travel agent is an antiques dealer at Rummel Creek, where KayDee, Vicki and Connie sell their stuff!).

The train's dining car waiter had an attitude and we were warned by Jean Dixon to not dare spill anything on the paper napkin spread across the tablecloth. We braved the man's wrath long enough to have breakfast and KayDee and Connie went to the dining car around midday to share a lunch of bread and frankfurters. Connie reported that it was actually quite tasty and by now, the waiter had mellowed a bit. We arrived in Budapest around 2:30 or 3:00 p.m. Lynn and Emily took a cab to the ship as we waited for a van. And waited, and waited, and waited. A little old man who had helped us onto the train held us up for $25---long story. We just wanted him gone. Finally, just after Cam commandeered a van, our Uniworld guy showed up with printed instructions to pick us up at 4:30. Unfortunately, he didn't know exactly where the ship was docked (and the ship's phone number had been disconnected--the driver's cell phone was on the fritz to add to the drama of it all). We spotted the ship ourselves and directed him to it.

The ship held about 140 passengers and has all the amenities of the big ships (our swimming pool was a little small however...a child's plastic wading pool). The crew was comprised of many young Eastern Europeans and Norwegians. The food and beverage manager became close as we communicated with eyebrow lifts and exaggerated eye movements. He was gay as can be and---well, as Connie said - he would have been the perfect shopping companion. It's always good to get on with the food and beverage guy. We learned that his name is Olaf. We dined and gazed at the scenery outside...Buda rising to the West and Pest languishing to the East. (Until 1873, *Budapest* was two cities; Buda with the hills and Pest on a plateau.) Think of full enticing breasts and iron-flat stomach and you will then have an idea of how beautiful the city really is.

The weather on June 5 was 60° and overcast. Some call *Budapest* the Paris of the East; others say it more closely resembles Vienna. The settlement that is now *Budapest* (pronounced Buda-Peshed) dates back to 2,000 BC and has been under many influences, so both descriptions have validity. Down river, we could see the graceful *Lánchíid* (Chain Bridge) that finally connected the two sides of the city in the early 1900s. There are now other bridges in place including Liberty Bridge and Elizabeth Bridge. They all looked very impressive and stately at night. We were lucky to be there on this post war night. During WWII, the Germans damaged over 80% of the city, and destroyed all of the bridges. Later, the Soviets rolled into the city center during 1956 and the Hungarians fought them. The next day, we would see evidence of battle in the form of bullet holes in a building on Castle Hill.

Sleeping late was verboten on this cruise. Breakfast began at 7:00 AM and tours started at 8:30. Our bus first took us to the *Pest* side and we are given a few moments to look around Heroes' Square. It contains the *Millennium Monument* that was built in 1896 to mark the 1,000th anniversary of the seven Magyar tribes settling at this spot. The center column has equestrian statues of the tribal chieftains at the base and at the top is the archangel Gabriel. Legend has it that Gabriel appeared to the future King Stephen in a dream bearing a crown. Behind the column is a colonnade of some of the great people in Hungarian history. We walked past the *Vásárcsarnok* (The Great Market Hall) that was built in 1897. We wanted to go inside this fabulous food market but, alas, it was closed. We were looking forward to shopping because we were told Budapest is a great place to shop, but here we were in Budapest and today (Monday) was a holiday. Dang it!

As we toured, via bus, our guide gave us little samplings of information such as the fact that *Budapest* was the first city on the Continent to have a subway. It was built in 1896; London's was completed two years earlier. Our guide also told us that there are two types of pedestrians...fast or flat! The movie *Evita* was shot mostly (80%) in *Budapest* and the rest was shot in *Munich*. We learned that Hungarians are 65% Catholic, and that the old name for the Castle District was the Water District.

Connie wrote, "We then toured the Parliament building; which is a distinctive feature of the city's skyline. It is one of the biggest houses of parliament in the world. Its architectural style is patterned after the British Parliament. The holy crown of Hungary is displayed there and they say it's worth going inside to look at the richly decorated interior. We'll have to go by what they say, because we couldn't do the tour unless Parliament is in session. Another disappointment!"

We passed by but did not enter the Synagogue at *Dohany* Street. It was quite beautiful and is the largest Synagogue in *Budapest*. Our guide told us that the Russians re-painted the top of the Synagogue's towers with the Russian colors of black and gold. We saw the State Opera House, the *Pest* Concert Hall and the National Museum. All closed! So, we saw them all from a distance!

After touring parliament, we were scheduled to have tea at one of Hungary's top rated restaurants. The *Gundel* restaurant was founded in 1879 and the founder's heirs eventually moved the restaurant to the current location and helped it achieve worldwide acclaim. In 1991, Ronald Lauder (of the Estée Lauder family) and George Lang, a gastronomic writer, bought the restaurant, promising to return it to its former glory. It has since been named one of the ten best restaurants in the world. It is also famous for its *Gundel* Pancake. The recipe was created by *Karoly Gundel* 100 years ago and is filled with rum, raisins, lemon rind and walnuts; then topped with a chocolate sauce and fried in the oven or flambéed at the table. (go to <www.gundel.hu/ gundel en php> for sample menus, etc.). The *Gundel* was also closed for the holiday. Darn!

We did get to tour the oldest part of *Budapest*, called District 1 or the First District; the oldest area of the city. Buildings and

medieval homes dating as far back as the 13th Century had been restored (cobblestone streets completed the look). Castle Hill, as it is called, was the site of the final German stand in 1944. By the end of the fighting, all of Castle Hill's palaces, mansions and churches were destroyed. Architectural plans from medieval times had been preserved and the entire complex was reconstructed. The National Gallery, the Royal Palace, Fisherman's Bastion and Matthias Church (where Franz Joseph I was crowned King in 1867) all comprise part of District I. Matthias Church was founded 700 years ago, but most of the structure was from the 19th century. A new and modern Hilton Hotel is nearby and many think its modernism destroys the site's panache. Fisherman's Bastion offers a breathtaking panoramic view of *Pest* across the Donau and faces the commanding spires of the Houses of Parliament. Fisherman's Bastion has seven turrets to commemorate the seven "Magyar" tribes that founded Hungary in 896 A.D. We watched some falconers, took pictures and gawked as though we were in tourist heaven. We were then given about 45 minutes to do some shopping in the few surrounding shops and in two small street markets. Connie bought a ceramic bracelet and a large red flower made by an artist selling her own wares. She, too quickly, bought a pin as she was returning to the bus, but when she looked at it more carefully later, decided it was made in China, not Hungary.

Our guided tour didn't last too long, so we had the afternoon to ourselves. We, not being able to walk very far, inspected the neighborhood near the dock, a very busy place of both commerce and dwelling. The ship has a shuttle boat that took the rest of our gang to the *Pest* side of the city. KayDee, Jean, Vicki, Cam and Connie gave themselves a walking tour that turned out to be quite pleasant, although the shops that they would have really liked to have browsed in were closed.

Our Captain (Jord Zwaal, a Dutchman) looked 16 years old but was about to turn 29 on June 6th ... but was still pretty young for a Captain. We were introduced to the crew as we sipped complimentary libations before adjourning to the dining room for a scrumptious meal that was beautifully prepared and artfully presented. Olaf was a little frustrated because he was short a waiter or two. Some had gone on leave and hadn't bothered to return, so he had to oversee things and wait on several tables too. More eyebrow lifts! After dinner we were treated to a Hungarian Operetta in the Lounge. Then our ship departed for our next venture into Hungary and we went to sleep.

We awoke to see a small shanty and a house with a couple of other buildings. The shanty is obviously a shop set up just for river cruisers like we. There is only farmland in the surrounding area. Following breakfast, several buses arrived to take us on a short ride to *Kalocsa*, a small but historically important town. *Kalocsa* was founded by Hungary's first King, St. Stephen (King Stephen the Saint). It is located in the southern part of the Great Hungarian Plain. Throughout the centuries, its land has been occupied by intruders and the town has been burned to the ground a number of times. The last time much of the town was destroyed by a fire was in 1875. Its small thatched houses also had to suffer the frequent floods and the drainage of backwaters and marshes. In fact, *Kalocsa* was once at the banks of the Danube but the riverbed has changed over the years moving away from the town. The Danube it is now about four miles east of *Kalocsa*.

On the way to our first stop, we saw beautiful, well-tended, fields and some small orchards. At the outskirts of the town there were some well-kept, modest homes and a few neighborhood businesses. We saw women hoeing in the fields as they grow cabbages, sunflowers, wheat, etc.

The soil appears to be quite fertile. We were soon amongst the 18,000 inhabitants of Kalosca. All the houses had fences. (There are no fences in the countryside and fields appear to be endless.) Our guide told us that there are no guns to protect from thieves, so people keep mean dogs instead. The farmers bring their crops to the "*publica*" (co-op) where they can sell, buy, process or dry their products. There are also markets each Wednesday and Saturday where organic products were sold to the public. The guide pointed out a jail for women. She said there were about 300 prisoners there from all over the country.

We also learned that the Communists wanted to industrialize the agricultural production in Hungary and wanted to plant rice and cotton...but the climate did not support those crops. While the Russians occupied Hungary, they wanted only Russian spoken, but they didn't teach it well. Our guide's mother could recite, by heart, the Russian history of Lenin and Stalin in perfect Russian, but could not ask for a drink of water in the language.

Our first stop was the Bishop's Palace, home to one of Hungary's then four archbishops of the Roman Catholic Church. The original building looked like a palace but it is now a relatively plain three-winged baroque style building with a copper roof that has turned green. The building itself was painted a very bright mustard color because the buildings were built during the reign of Maria Theresa and yellow was the Queen's favorite color. Dogs protected the Bishop's garden behind the Palace, so we couldn't walk through it. Photos on the web show that the garden has been pretty much unchanged for at least 60 years. It is said to be home to a number of valuable plants. Inside the Palace, across from the residences, was a fabulous old library (the Archbishop's Library). No cameras were allowed. It contained 150,000 volumes and a collection of medals and coins. All the books were bound in similar leather. It was interesting that the windows were open. Someone asked about the humidity control and the answer was somewhat vague, but whatever they did, it was obviously working. Best of all, the library could be used for doing research.

Next, we went to the Paprika Museum (kind of a dud), but it was interesting because paprika (made from sweet peppers) is so necessary to spice food of the region. It is also called "red gold" (*piros arany*) and is an obviously important product to Hungarians. We were disappointed that we didn't see rows of colorful houses with huge multiple strings of bright red peppers hanging from the eaves, as had been shown in pre-trip photos. However, the museum itself exhibited a good example of wall-painting (called *Pingálás*). A beautiful and brightly color floral border was hand painted along the edge of the ceiling. We were told that paprika, depicted in the floral border, came here via Christopher Columbus in the 15th century. At first it was considered just an ornamental plant that only the poor people consumed. Later it was used as an herb that could have been responsible for curing cholera and scurvy. It was finally cultivated in the 19th century and, in the 20th century, was finally taken to market where it is used in cosmetics and to fight mosquitoes and is reputed to have a "*Viagra*" type property. While this museum was a little disappointing, our next stop was not!

We traveled further into the countryside to Hungary's "horse country", called the *Puszta*. We were greeted at a ranch by locals wearing native costumes and by some young horsemen on beautiful steeds---the horseman carried long whips in their hands. The attendants offered us a local alcoholic drink. We quickly learned that salt and bread or some combination thereof is offered to visitors before a meal or an event. The young horsemen were wearing rather strange costumes. Their hats were flared on either side and their coats and hats are a sort of blue gray color. The riders are called *Czikos* (Czikos, the cowboys of the puszta) and are representative of the Magyars, a warrior tribe of horsemen from the steppes of central Asia that settled in Hungary in the 9th century. We settled together in the bleachers and the *Czikos* were off...cracking their whips so loudly that it sounded like gunshots. They showed how the horses sat and the *Czikos* leaned against them, pretending to sleep; and performed other tricks of horseman-like bravado. One guy on the burro acted as the comic relief. The little burro was also well trained. We quickly realized that these were expert horsemen. KayDee and Connie were summoned from their front row seats to be 'whipped' by the cowboys to demonstrate their amazing abilities with rawhide. Before leaving, we took a wild and fast wagon ride and did a little shopping at the tables set up on our way out. Painted eggs, photos of the horsemen, paprika, local honey and some homemade items were for sale.

We then returned to *Kalocsa* to look inside the beautiful church next to the Archbishop's Palace. An organ concert was under way. Most people were sleeping, so it's a good thing that the organist was behind and above us. The Jezsuita church was beautiful architecturally and was tastefully, yet modestly, appointed. The Palace, the Church and the monastery abut a lovely little park and a monument to World War I heroes; and there is also a statue of St. Stephen. To see some beautiful photos of this great little Hungarian town, go to <members.tripod.com/ gdraskoy/Kalocsa/ Recent_photos.html>. There you will see photos of the city as it is and as it was. It's a charming little website with many photos by Hungarian photographer George Draskoy. It even shows the house his family used to live in.

We next wound our way back about four miles to our ship. It began to rain on the already swelling and flooding

Danube. We haven't a care because we had good weather this morning and there's plenty to do on board; like sip afternoon tea, enjoy a lecture about tomorrow's adventure, and relax as our pianist, Matthew, treated us to a short concert. We also celebrated our Captain's 29th birthday as we lazily push downstream to Belgrade, Serbia. It was Wednesday, June 7, 2006 - with 68° and Partly Cloudy predicted.

The next morning we could be somewhat leisurely as our first tour wasn't until 1:00 p.m. This gave us time to attend a lecture on "*Serbia and Croatia and the legacy of Yugoslavia*" hosted by a guest lecturer, Mr. Manole. We also had an early lunch so that we could be ready to tour *Belgrade* (also called Beograd). The weather was partly cloudy and the clouds rained on us pretty heftily. *Belgrade* is one of Europe's oldest cities. Its 2,500-year history is fraught with invaders and conquerors of every description: Huns, Sarmatians, Ostrogoths, Avars, Slavs, Romans, Ottoman Turks, the Germans, and most recently, the Communists. We got an eyeful as we saw for ourselves what our lecturer had been talking about. The *Kalemegdan Fortress*, where many attempts were made to repel invaders, now languished on high, at a point where three rivers merge, like a tired old watchdog for the city's 1.6 million inhabitants. Eighty-six percent of the population were Serbs. Many have called *Belgrade* "the moodiest of all the capital cities in the Balkans" and this melancholy can be felt as we toured the city. We chalked it up to the weather, but later learned that many others have felt this way while here - rain or shine. Many buildings were dilapidated and there were few historical monuments or things of archaeological interest. But, considering all it's been through, it still had a style of its own. *Belgrade* has been under some form of attack 54 times since AD1, or every 37 years on average.

We drove past Republic Square, the National Museum, Parliament House, Town Hall and the Dom Cathedral. We also saw many remaining buildings that had been bombed out...a reminder that this city has never ceased to be a prime target for just about everyone (the last being NATO bombers during the Kosovo crisis of 1999). They showed us the "Upscale Living Quarters" where high-ranking Communist leaders lived, and contrasted that set up with the Communist housing projects where they made the citizenry live. We saw the same thing in St. Petersburg, so it's not such a shock. Our daily program summed it up, "... the Communist housing projects for the citizens of Belgrade starkly staring at us forlornly from across the Donau." We saw Tito's Memorial (his wife was still living because she was about 35 years younger than he) and visited the St. Sava Cathedral, now under construction on the site where it is believed that St. Sava's remains were burned by the Turk *Sinan Pasha* in 1595. It was the third largest Eastern Orthodox church in the world. Money for the construction was not coming from the government, the church or locals, but rather from Serbs working in other countries and sending money home for the cause.

On March 9, 1991 massive demonstrations were held against Serbian President Slobodan Milosevic, but tanks were brought in to squelch the uprising. More demonstrations were held in 2000; finally causing his ousting. Our guide told us that 1.5 million demonstrated near the Parliament building, then headed to the same TV station that was bombed in 1999 by NATO. She said that every evening when the news would come on TV and Milosevic would speak, people would open their windows and bang pots and pans to show they didn't want to listen to anything he had to say. The average salary here was about $350 a month and private secondary schools cost about $6,000 a year. They have good doctors but poor equipment. The Prince and Princess are helping with some of the charities.

Our next stop was for refreshments at the Hotel Majestic and we were offered the opportunity to either go on with the tour of the Fortress or to shop on *Mihajilova* Street. Pat and I and Jean opted for the tour, while the antiquers began their slightly wet sojourn through the Serbian streets and shops. Connie tells the story: "I was intent upon finding a tee shirt before we left town. Vicki, Cam and KayDee were very patient as we got close to the end of the shopping street. I had yet to find a lousy tee shirt. A street vendor directed us to about four blocks back from where we just came from. There, I found the coolest tee shirt ever! It's black and white with a big bold *Belgrade* running vertically, and running horizontally was a listing of all the major sites in the city. The shoppers then traipsed back to the ship over wet streets and alternating mist and rain. We all had to pass through another ship tied up side-by-side to get to ours. Hold it! What's this? This ship's gift shop was so much better than ours! It had things we'd love to buy but, alas, it is closed to us. Darn."

Reunited on board, we all then settled down in the cocktail lounge and enjoyed a drink to remove the chill of the rain. Serbia was slightly depressing with all of the bombed out buildings and the wetness. It would probably look better on a sunny day. And, in ten years, hopefully for the citizens, it may be a free and vibrant hub of positive growth and activity. They deserve it.

On Thursday June 8, 2006, we were cruising down the Danube and headed to the 'Iron Gates'. It was 64°, with a chance of rain. The Purser and our Cruise Director, Hans, alerted us to the fact that some of the various customs officials are quite serious about their jobs and don't mind detaining ships or disturbing passengers in the middle of the night. Sure enough, we stopped in *Veliko Gradiste* for customs clearance. It seems as though one passenger had failed to return his passport to the Purser so a "face check" was ordered. Passports, later returned to their owners, were collected. Then the customs officials knocked on each door and matched the "face" to the photo. The crew was laughing about the time this happened in the middle of the night and passengers had to assemble in the lounge in their nightclothes. Without makeup, some of the women didn't quite match their photo I.D. and a few men were balder than in their photos too, making the face check a little harder than they had thought. Our "face check" didn't slow us down much but it made for an earlier start to a day of leisurely cruising than one would have preferred. Our Captain returned from the customs office where he had to submit additional documents. He smiled and waved a hearty 'hello' for our cameras.

We gathered for breakfast first, and proceeded to the top deck to observe the Iron Gates experience. The gates operate in much the same fashion as the Panama Canal and it was a fascinating experience for us because it is on a much smaller scale than the big ships that go through the canal; and it was all so close. You could reach out and touch the sides of the gates. We now had sea-time to chat about our fellow travelers, who by and large were most compatible. There didn't seem to be a grump amongst the group. Everyone was interesting and all were well traveled (this is not a "first vacation" kind of joy-ride). There was a young man in his late 30s or early 40s who had left his wife and kids behind so he could take this trip with his 70+ year old dad. They were from Canada and were as fun as can be. The young man was quick with a quip or funny observation and his Dad was a joy. Also, there were two women from California who left their husbands at home in order to travel with their mother. They told us that they also did this when their dad was alive--a true blood relative's only vacation once a year. They had been everywhere, so it seemed. Their mom was a live wire too. The youngest passenger was about 12 years old and he was traveling with his dermatologist dad. His dad took each kid on a "just you and me" trip when each child was about this age. The boy didn't seem to mind being with all we old people and was very well behaved. We also got a running commentary of events from the Wheelhouse as we passed through the gates. We no sooner got through the gates when the rain started. But, we had lucked out again weather-wise and we enjoyed a lazy afternoon on board ship reading or napping or just chatting with new friends. Nice way to go!

At 4 p.m., we dressed for high tea. Chefs had prepared wonderful cakes and cookies to go with our tea, Earlier there had been a lecture about modern Bulgaria by a guest lecturer. After tea, he talked about the various types of architecture we had seen and would be seeing. Then, he updated us regarding our first day in Bulgaria as we visited *Veliko Tarnovo* and *Arbanassi*. We went back to our cabins, and Pat and I tried for a short nap. As dinner time approached, we arose to dress; and then strange things began happening to me! As I stood up to put on my dinner jacket, I suddenly felt as if I were floating around six inches above the floor. People appeared shadowy as I started down the hallway to the dinner compartment. Pat pulled me back into our cabin and forced me onto the bed, while she called for help. I was feeling no pain and vaguely remembered a previous similar experience with a hyperglycemic (low blood sugar) episode. The trouble was that I, a full-fledged Diabetic, was too 'high' and too happy to pass this info along. Everyone diagnosed a stroke!

Pat summoned this ship's doctor to show him a list of my medications. The bad news was that the drugs have other names in Europe, and nobody knew what they were or did. By now, our friends were seated for dinner when they learned of my problem. They reached out and found some physicians on board. Two were retired doctors from Houston, but Connie was told that the ship had requested that the doctors not reveal themselves. Probably some sort of liability for both the passenger and the ship; and that it was the ship's doctor who is responsible for assessment/ treatment. Word spread quickly about my mishap and everyone expressed concern. One passenger said, "pass the list of medicines around and have people who take the same thing tell you why they take it. This way the doctor will have a better idea of what problems I might be experiencing." Great idea! Cam jumped into action and went from table to table gathering information. One nurse, presumably gay because she wore a man's suit and tie to dinner, was especially helpful. Cam continued to assist Pat in any way he could and to be attentive and unobtrusive.

Enter the ship's Doctor, Bogdan Mutu (a young Romanian; destined to become our friend and visit us in California). He was very caring and thought that I might have to go to a hospital at our next stop near medical facilities: *Rouse*. Pat was frantic because she would be alone with a sick husband in a foreign country without any money and with no credit card. Bogdan soothed her and stood by watching me. Our friends told her not to worry about money - they would loan it to her. In the meantime, I felt fine but couldn't convince people that I was OK. After 10:00 PM, when the doctor had left for the evening, Connie paid us a short visit and gave me a good night hug. I told her what I was now sure of - it was not a stroke but that I had let my blood sugar get out of whack by not following my normal Diabetes regimen. I told Connie that my biggest regret was that I might not be able to celebrate her 60th birthday "big day" on June 9, if

Bogdan wouldn't permit me to go ashore. Connie told me that was the least thing to consider and relayed to us how practically every one on board had come by the table to inquire as to my condition. Genuine concern by strangers!

The next morning found us docked to visit two Bulgarian towns, *Veliko Tarnovo* and *Arbanassi* on a 74 degree, partly sunny day. I felt and looked good. We all had breakfast together, but Pat was still concerned that it could have been a mini-stroke. So, with Bogdan's urging, we opted to spend the day onboard where the crew gave us wonderful care and attention. The rest of our gang took seats on the buses for a trip to *Veliko Tarnovo* and would re-join the boat down-river. The area they explored had its own hard and lengthy history. The town was named Tarnovo after two brothers whose last name was Tarnovgrad. The brothers helped lead a rebellion against the Byzantine rulers. By the 13th century, the town was nearly as important to the region as Constantinople. They had about 200 years of prosperity before the Turks destroyed the fortress and took over rule in 1393. The Bulgarian culture and nationalism began to be revived in the mid 1800s. In 1878, the Burrians liberated Tarnovo from the Turks. Here was where the present Bulgarian Constitution was written. Bulgaria declared full independence in 1908. In l965, the city was renamed *Veliko* ("greater") *Tarnovo*.

As they observed the countryside, nice and comfy in modern buses, they saw people working the fields by hand. Horse- or donkey- drawn carts were hauling hay or other goods from the fields to the small towns. Fields were plowed by horse-drawn 19th century variety plows. They were delivered to a good-sized hotel in greater downtown *Veliko Turnovo* and had a quick refreshment and given 20 minutes to shop in the adjoining gift shop. A regional product seems to be rose soap, rose cologne, rose hand lotion, etc. Connie bought a tee-shirt with the town name and a beautiful rose on it. This is part of Bulgaria's Valley of the Roses, which produces over 80% of the rose essence for the world's perfume industries. They wandered across the street and walked up a steep cobblestone path past tiny 'Mom and Pop' shops. They found they were walking along Gurko Street in the *Samodivene* Market, which was rebuilt to re-establish the Bulgarian National Revival period. One shop made pots and pans, in another, a young man and his dad made wooden toys, spoons and other wood items - like a spoon with a whistle carved at the end of the handle. Nearby was the *Forty Martyrs* Church, a medieval Eastern Orthodox Church that was built in 1230. The church housed some of the Bulgarian Empire's most significant historical records including Omurtag's Column, Asen's Column and the Border Column, all from the reign of Khan Krum.

They departed *V-T*, and the buses took them higher into the Balkan mountain range. They were headed for *Arbanassi*, just a few miles beyond *V-T*. There were some very nice homes and they were told that it is now a mountain retreat for wealthier Bulgarians; and that 90 churches, homes and monasteries in the village are protected as cultural monuments by the government. *Arbanassi*'s normal population was at that time around 310. It is famed for its austere houses which resemble minor fortresses on the outside with high, solid walls and heavy gates, and secret hiding-places. But the homes are supposedly spacious and comfortable and richly decorated and nicely furnished on the inside.

They first visited the oldest of Arbanassi's five churches; The *Birth of Christ* Church, built from 1637 to 1649. It is dug into the ground and has hidden cupolas and no belfry. The building is curved almost like a cave or an old root cellar. The walls are covered with over 3,500 stunningly realistic figures and Biblical scenes, painted by unknown artists throughout the ages. It is thought that the traveling artists were paid to do the art by the more wealthy inhabitants of Arbanassi. Everyone stood for the long church service; men on one side of the room and women on the other. There were no musical instruments played; there were only blended human voices singing. They heard a demonstration by an impressive quartet of singers. They noted that people were not tall back then, since the top of Cam's head almost hit the ceiling.

Next, they walked down the road a bit to *Sarafkina Kashta* mansion that was once the home of a wealthy Turkish merchant in the mid 1800s. The home was quite spacious and it was noted that there were indoor toilets (upstairs and down). Connie couldn't remember if it was a one hole or a two hole potty, but upstairs you would sit on the wooden seat and let her rip down to the hole in the ground two stories below. Probably didn't make the house smell all that good but they might have had something for that, who knows. There was also a special room for expectant mothers. Downstairs was now a gift shop. They then walked a bit further and had lunch. They were greeted by a smiling young women who offered them bread and salt before entry into the restaurant. While enjoying a delicious three-course lunch, they were entertained by musicians and dancers dressed in traditional costumes. The courtyard where the entertainment took place was surrounded on three sides by the meandering restaurant; the fourth side housing live animals, including a cantankerous donkey.

After lunch, they returned to V-T and were given an option: Shopping or visiting the *Tsarevets Fortress* that was being restored. They were told that the Byzantines built the original structure and it had to be rebuilt several times. The Turks finished off its destruction in 1393. The guide said that the views of the surrounding mountains and town make the

long walk worthwhile. Their dilemma; do they shop or do they walk around a reproduced fort? Jean chose the Fortress while the antiquers elected to shop. The bus dropped them off back at that great Gurko Street *Samodivene* Market that they had stumbled onto earlier. The antiquers were overjoyed and wildly went about their business!

After the passengers had departed from the ship earlier in the morning, it left its shoreside mooring and proceeded down river to the next stop: *Rousse*. Here, it collected the sightsee-ers from their buses. There is a Bridge of Friendship over the Danube that connects *Rousse* with the town of *Gyurgevo*, Romania. *Rousse* now had fewer than half of its previous inhabitants (current population at trip time was around 180,000). Seems it was difficult to find a job there. But, it is a beautiful city with large promenades and many parks that are unfortunately juxtaposed against Soviet communist-style apartment complexes that were just as depressing here as they are everywhere else. If you want to see some beautiful photos of *Rousse* go to www.4windstravel.com/shows/danube2003/rousse.html. **You can also see/read some interesting stuff by going to** www.geotimes.org/aug05/Travels0805.htm - **"Stone Sleuthing in Rousse, Bulgaria" by Edward Monroe. Here is an advisory that Connie found on the 4winds web site:**

"*Rousse* is the largest Bulgarian port on the Danube. The Roman Emperor Vespasian founded a river port here for the Roman Danube fleet. It was destroyed in the 6th century and remained insignificant until the end of the 19th century. The city has played an important role in the struggle for liberation from the "Turkish Yoke" (Ottoman Empire), which succeeded in 1878. The town once again declined under Communist rule. Bulgaria was long a friend of Russia because Russia helped liberate Bulgaria from the Turks."

Reunited with our friends, we relaxed and had cocktails before dressing for dinner and Connie's birthday celebration, which we planned while they were touristing. KayDee and Connie walked into the dining room together, and to her surprise, there was a huge bouquet of long stemmed pink roses and white lilies on the table and everyone sang 'Happy Birthday'. Gifts were distributed. Vicki and Cam had looked everywhere to find a birthday card and went to great lengths to get flowers delivered to the ship. Both the Captain and guide Hans, came by to wish her a Happy Birthday. Her eyebrow raising friend, Olaf, gave her a double kiss. Lynn and Emily sent a nice note and a bottle of wine to our table. Pat and I had composed a poem (below) and I read it to all...then sang a naughty little ditty (*Suzanne was a Lady with plenty of* class, etc. – with Connie in place of Suzanne) from my soon-to-be published book, "*Songs My Mother Never Sang To Me*." KayDee has also presented a poem. Jean gave her a fun gift of a ladybug in a wooden box whose bug's legs moved like crazy. The ship brought a fabulous birthday cake to the table. It was the end of a wonderful day for Connie- and the rest of us.

Poem From Pat & Bob...to Connie

When you are sixty, you are like a pixie
Neither young or old,
When you are Connie and arrive at sixty
Your world has just begun to unfold,
She's been traveling down life's byways,
On land, and ocean and highways,
And has made friends by the gross,
We met her on a liner going to Chile or Chiner,
And she said her name was Vass or Voss,

We like her spunk and her aversion to junk
And her love of anything wry,
We want to keep traveling with Connie forever,
And never have to say goodbye.

From KayDee... "Ode to Connie"

Today is the day of your birth,
Good wishes we offer to you!
A lifetime filled with mirth,
Lots of tee shirt shopping to do!

Arrival in Prague brought great excitement to you,
To find that elusive tee shirt,
What were you to do?

As you work your way through the Balkans,
Fertile valleys, mountains and hills,
You've seen castles, Churches and bastions,
Rolling down the Danube has brought many thrills.

Budapest was just lovely,
Sausages you had,
From Castle Hill and Fisherman's Bastion,
The view was not bad.

On to Kalocsa where paprika abounds,
But you liked the wine,
And those cowboys you found.

In Belgrade the weather was rainy and sad,
But you had a mission

A tee shirt to be had!

So on with your quest,
Just several blocks more,
The history of Budapest,
Is on the tee shirt you wore.

Don't think of it as work,
Just think of it as sport,
More tee shirts ahead,
So on to the next port!

The alarm is sounding,
Its time for a face check,
Get your passports ready,
What do you expect?

Bleary-eyed passengers,
All dressed in their robes,
Rudely awakened,
Checking passports we're told.

On to the castle some handicrafts to buy,
Some candy, some coffee, some tee shirts,
But why? Connie won't soon forget that Bulgarian song,
To nod the wrong way was right and the right way was
wrong!

I need just one more,
Can't you understand, she said,
I'll shop 'til I drop,
And collect 'til I'm dead!

A trip through the Iron Gates,

To Romania we go,
In search of more tee shirts,
For Connie to show.

So on to Bucharest,
With shirts on her mind,
Happy Birthday to Connie,
Good Wishes, Good Times!

By the next morning, Saturday, June 10, 2006, we arrived at the port city of *Cernavoda*, Romania, which served the Black Sea resorts of *Constanta* and *Mamaia*. It was 76° and Partly Cloudy. We had a full day's excursion to *Constanta* planned for today. We were now located halfway between Istanbul, Turkey and Odessa, Ukraine. *Constanta* is the second largest city in Romania and is also the oldest city in the country, having been inhabited for over 26 centuries. They said Greek traders set up shop here in the 6th century B.C. and called the place *Tomis*. There is a much more romantic, but probably untrue, story that says it was founded by the survivors of a battle with Jason's Argonauts following his capture of the Golden Fleece. (for more of the Greek lore on the subject, visit <en.wikipedia.org/wiki/Golden_fleece>.)

Tomis was later renamed to commemorate the Byzantine Emperor Constantine. There was a statue in the old town square (*Plata Ovidiu*) that paid homage to Ovid (a poet in the first century A.D.). Ovid was exiled to this, the farthest Roman outpost, after he wrote *Ars Amatoria* (The Art of Making Love). Our daily information guide said that Emperor Augustus did not like the poem or the subject matter and punished Ovid for writing the witty ditty; or it could have been that Ovid had an affair with one of Augustus' relatives. The real reason for the banishment has been lost. His writings revealed, however, that despite the natural beauty of this area, Ovid longed to be in Rome and was miserable in this place.

Constanta overcame its dismal centuries of occupation and finally, in the 1900s, became the seaside resort of choice for the rich and famous. But, WW2 and the years of Communist oppression took their toll for the next fifty years. It was just now coming back into its own. Thus, it was nice to see it before it takes on the appearance of the French or Italian Riviera. The city itself now had a long way to go and was probably one of the less clean and less architecturally exciting cities in Europe. It had a more third world look that any of the major cities we've visited.

Our first stop was the Archaeological Museum that adjoins some ancient Roman ruins. One highlight was the mosaic floor that is surprisingly intact – possibly restored. Among the other exhibits were twenty-four 2nd Century Roman statues that were found under the city's old train station in 1962; including the serpent *Glykon* who had been carved from a single block of marble. We left our buses and walked through the neighborhood where children (probably Gypsy's) were begging for money. They were playing and happy before they saw us; then their expressions changed to sorry and sad. Later we learned that Gypsy's originated in India and now comprise about 10% of the Romanian population.

The neighborhood we walked through was not in good repair but was interesting nonetheless. The iron doors on residences were fabulous. One had large spiders in an S design. Laundry hung on lines from the balconies above. The homes were usually no more than two or three stories high. No way of finding out how many people live in one dwelling. We passed by the *Mahmoud II Mosque* that was built in 1910. We were told that the structure was a mixture of Byzantine and Romanian architecture; it looked beautiful from our somewhat distant vantage point. We proceeded to an important church, the *Orthodox Cathedral*, and arrived just as a baby was being christened. The guide told us to go on in and to even snap a few photos. The baby's relatives were taking photos; one using a camcorder.

We continued our walk and got our first glimpse of the Black Sea. It was a beautiful aqua blue color. A large and beautiful white stone building, straight ahead, was jutting out on a small peninsula. It was a Casino, but didn't appear to be operating. To the left was the beginning of a long combination seaside walkway/sea wall, which we figured must go to the beach, located to the left at the end of our line of sight. When we walked to the rear side of the Casino, there were tables indicating that there was a restaurant housed somewhere inside. There were no diners at this hour. Perhaps they came later in the day or evening. We re-boarded our Bus and drove downtown for a brief shopping opportunity. We didn't see much of interest. There were some large retail stores, but their window displays didn't hold any fascination. We stopped at a couple of small bakeries but didn't buy anything. We then rode a few miles to an ocean side resort, called *Mamaia*, for a closer look at the Black Sea. Following lunch, we strolled along the beach and rolled up our pants legs so that we could get a first hand taste of the Black Sea. We made a memory and a picture that we have saved for history: Jean Dixon, knee deep in the Black Sea, holding up her hands in triumph!

There was an aerial tram ride nearby that would have given us a more interesting view, but we feared that it would take longer than our allotted time. Connie searched in vain for a souvenir shop that at least sold a tee shirt. But there were none; only some rather uninteresting local crafts and not many of those. Our guide sheet told us that we should consider buying a suede-like hat made from a type of fungus. Ugh! We figured that it must have been a little too early in the season before the resort got into full swing.

Upon returning to the ship, we prepared for our "Captain's Farewell Cocktail" party in the lounge. So soon to think about leaving! Much too soon if you were to ask most of us; the ship had been quite comfortable. After dinner we were treated to another local talent show of Romanian Folk Music. Now, we had to get packed and leave our bags outside our doors bright and early, so that we could complete our trip with a 2-night hotel stay and a couple of day excursions in and around *Bucharest*. On Sunday, June 11, 2006 we arrived at *Oltenita*, Romania, the ship's final port and proceeded via bus to *Bucharest* on a 76° and 'Partly Cloudy' day. It was hard for us to contemplate that we had spent six days on the ship and were already leaving, taking only our memories and personal items with us.

Bucharest was all they told us it would be and more. It was a bustling city with legendary traffic snarls. If you thought a trip would take you 30-minutes, better, allow one-hour or more. The city was a nice mix of old and new. We were first taken to the Palace of the People (*Casa Poporului*) which housed the Romanian Parliament and now has been renamed 'The Palace of the Parliament'. At first glance the building was of an overwhelming size. Then we learned that it is the second largest building in the world; second only to our own Pentagon. It is 12 stories high in the center with four underground levels that cannot be seen as you stand outside (the four underground levels were in various stages of completion). It has 1,100 rooms. It is estimated that one million cubic meters of marble from *Transylvania* was used during construction. The building contained 480 chandeliers, 1,409 ceiling lights and mirrors plus 200,000 of square meters of woolen carpets. The rooms were so big that machines were put inside the building in order to weave some of the carpets. Nuns had hand embroidered

trim on the enormous draperies that cover the windows (easily 30 feet high).

It is said that because of the large amount of marble used for this one building, that marble tombstones were not made for several years. Effectively, the building, due to its immense size, cuts the city in half - an urban planner's nightmare. Construction of the Palace and the Central Civic surrounding area required demolishing about one-fifth of the historic districts of Bucharest. The avenue in front of the building looks conspicuously like the Champs-d'Elysées in Paris, which is what it was patterned after; only it was built to be longer than the 'Champs'. There is even a Triumphal Arch that looks very much like the Arc de Triomph in Paris. But, as in most everything the mad Romanian dictator, Ceausescu did, the *Bucharest* 'Arch' falls short, when compared to the French version.

Why was this building erected in a country that was economically decimated under Communism? It's a sad yet fascinating story (*Excerpted from the internet...an account of recent Romanian history...*):

"Soviet troops were stationed on the territory of Romania and the country was abandoned by the Western powers, so the next stage brought a similar evolution to that of the other satellites of the Soviet Empire. The whole government was forcibly taken over by the Communists; the political parties were banned and their members were persecuted and arrested; King Michael I was forced to abdicate and that same day, the People's Republic was proclaimed (December 30, 1947). The single-party dictatorship was established, based on an omnipotent and omnipresent surveillance and repressive force. The industrial enterprises, the banks and transportation were nationalized (1948); agriculture was forcibly collectivized (1949-1962); the whole economy was developed according to five-year plans, the main goal being a Stalinist-type industrialization. Romania became a founding member of COMECON (1949) and of the Warsaw Treaty (1955)."

"At the death of Gheorghe Gheorghiu-Dej (1965), the Communist leader of the after-war epoch, the party leadership, which was later identified with that of the state as well, was monopolized by Nicolae Ceausescu. In a short period of time he managed to concentrate into his own hands (and those of a clan headed by his wife, Elena Ceausescu), all the power levers of the Communist party and of the state system. When Romania distanced itself from the USSR (this publicly inaugurated in the "Statement" of April 1964), the domestic policy was less rigid and there was some relaxing in the foreign policy (Romania was the only Warsaw Treaty member-state that did not intervene in Czechoslovakia in 1968). All this, as well as the political capital built on such a less Orthodox line, were used to consolidate Ceausescu's own position, and he took over complete power within the party and the state. The dictatorship of the Ceausescu family was one of the most absurd forms of totalitarianism in the 20th century Europe. It came with a personality cult that actually bordered on mental illness, and, as a result, caused, among other things, distortions in the economy, the degradation of the social and moral life, and the country's isolation from the international community. The country's resources were abusively used to build absurdly giant projects devised by the dictator's megalomania; this also contributed to a dramatic decline of the population's living standard and the deepening of the regime's crisis. Under these circumstances, the spark of revolt was initiated in *Timisoara* on December 16, 1989 and rapidly spread all over the country. On December 22 the dictatorship was overthrown with the sacrifice of over one thousand lives."

Our guide told us what life had been like under Ceausescu's reign. "My mother would leave at 4:00 AM to stand in line so that she could get an extra egg for me and my sister," said one guide. Another told us, "They built factories in absurd places...factories that did not have the raw materials necessary to produce much. Men would go to work and get drunk because they had nothing else to do."

On the same vast plain that the Palace was located on was another huge palace! This was the home of Madame Ceausescu. Apparently, it was verboten to tourists. We got another brief look at the city and made another stop at the cathedral of the Romanian Orthodox Patriarchy that was built in the 17th century and survived both communism and an earthquake. Since church was in session, it was difficult to see inside because of all the people. But, it looked interesting nonetheless. Next we went to the Restaurant *Pescarus*; which is located in a park-like setting next to one of many lakes in or around *Bucharest*. After lunch, we repaired to our Intercontinental Hotel, located in the heart of the city. Our room was large and the bathroom luxurious. We also had a nice balcony that provided us with a birds-eye view of the city. It was especially beautiful at night - *Bucharest* is known for its nightlife.

Early the next morning, in a cloudy and rainy environment, we were bused to the castle where Dracula used to hang out. We've never read Bram Stoker's book, *Dracula*, but you can, for free, at www.pagebypagebooks.com. As we left the city, we came to a point in the highway where all traffic was slowed as we passed through a chemical wash/spray of the bus. Apparently a recent outbreak of bird flu caused officials to take this action. We made a pit stop at a local café/tavern/quick shop. We then drove through the beautiful Carpathian Mountains and saw a number of interesting small villages and towns, seemingly devoted to winter sports. We finally arrived at a little tourist-type area at the foot of Bran Castle. The Castle, reachable by a long uphill walk to its entrance, was built in 1212 by the Knights of the Teutonic Order as a fortress. In the late 13th century it was taken over by the Saxons so that they could protect an important trade center (the City of *Brasov*). Pat and I decided that we couldn't do the uphill walk and so we remained in the area shopping center while the others braved the bite of Dracula.

There are many versions of the story of Dracula, but one that has stuck is that the character Dracula was based on Vlad the Impaler (son of Vlad Dracul). Vlad senior was dubbed a knight of the Dragon Order by the Hungarian king in the 1400s. All members of the order had a dragon on their coat of arms and that is how Vlad senior got the nickname Dracul (the Devil). His son, Vlad the Impaler used Draculya (the Devil's son) as his nickname. He was not referred to as "the Impaler" during his lifetime, only after he died in 1476. Young Vlad punished Saxon merchants and those who wanted to take his throne. Vlad ruled *Wallachia* between 1456 and 1462 and again in 1476. In 1462, after being defeated by the Turks, he took refuge in Hungary. In 1476, the Hungarian king, Matia Corvina, and a Moldavian prince, Stephen the Great, helped him regain the throne for a third time. Unfortunately for him, he held if for only a month before he was killed in a battle.

Impaling seemed to be Vlad's favorite way to invoke a slow death. One source says he killed over 40,000 people. Others, more favorable to his memory, say that he had a whole forest of sharp stakes with enemies' head on them. This spooked his enemies and his atrocities were recounted in books and pamphlets the Saxons produced and distributed, creating an even worse legacy for Vlad. Another version of the story is

found in a Romanian guidebook. It says that Bran Castle was built in the Middle Ages as a fortified customs station for an important commercial route. It was described in detail by the famous Venetian trader, *Pigafetta*, in his factual diary:

"The Castle takes its name from the village in which it stands, which in its turn was named by its ancient residents, referring either to *Bran*, the mythological Celtic giant whose severed head rendered its owner oblivious to the passage of time, or to *Bran*, the mythological owner of 'sacred time' that suspends the passing of 'profane time' ". The Guidebook continues; "What could be the connection between *Bran* and Dracula, the immortal vampire who lives by turning his victims into vampires? It is said that in the Middle Ages there were wolf men in the forests of Transylvania who were reputed to be immortal, and who had long canine teeth and faces completely covered with hair. The bite of these creatures would infect and sicken their victims. For this reason, once they were killed by the populace, they were decapitated and buried face down. In order to prevent them from resuscitating, stakes of ash wood were driven into their hearts from the back. It seems that Prince Vlad Tepes Dracul, an enthusiastic military commander and exterminator of invaders, was himself infected by the bite of one of these creatures, as it is said that he used to drink the blood of his victims as a ritual to celebrate his victories. Indeed, a tomb attributed to him contained a decapitated body in a face down position".

"In reality, Dracula's creator, writer Bram Stoker, had never been to Bran Castle or even to Romania. The version of the story received while our group was touring the castle says that fans of his books are said to have found the castle from Stoker's detailed description and claimed it to be the castle in which Dracula lived. Another version says that the author researched Bran Castle and its location and used it as the home for Count Dracula. It is possible that Stoker stumbled onto *Pigafetta*'s detailed description of the castle and used that in his book. Either way, Bran Castle is situated on the border between Transylvania and Wallachia and you can see why it was an ideal fortress. You can see someone coming for miles away!"

The Castle was – and still may be - owned by Princess Llenana of Romania who inherited it from her mother, Queen Marie. The castle was seized by the Communists in 1948, but was restored in the 1980s and became a tourist attraction after the Romanian Revolution of 1989. The legal heir had visited his castle just before our group arrived. He was the Princess's son, Dominic von Habsburg, who was an architect in New York City. The guides said that Habsburg was a very nice man and wanted to keep the castle as more of a Romanian historical site than a horror or Dracula attraction. It was also interesting to note that no one dressed as Dracula lurked about the grounds, although there were tee shirts with Dracula and blood available everywhere. The guide also mentioned that visiting Goths can really feel the evil vibes when they enter one room of the castle. That room used to be the home's Chapel. The guide said he just lets them think they're feeling the vibes and doesn't tell them it's a room for worship. Following our friend's Castle tour, we re-grouped for a short trip to our luncheon destination. Guess what was on the menu? Another version of goulash! Surprise!

We then left *Bran* and headed back towards *Bucharest*. After an hour or so, we stopped in *Sinaia* to visit a famous church and monastery. The Monastery was built from 1690 to 1695 and now houses the largest collection of religious art in Romania, mostly icons. Connie reported:

"I strolled around to the back of the monastery to a heavily wooded area because I could hear rushing water. Sure enough there was a cold mountain stream some feet below. Down the road a bit appeared to be some camper site. There was a street that made a couple of pretty sharp curves around the monastery, but the cars didn't seem to slow down; drivers treated the curves as a sport. I nearly got run over crossing the road. I wanted to see the people playing tennis at the courts across from the monastery. This would be a nice little town for a mountain vacation and there appeared to be some pretty fancy lodgings further down the road. I would later learn that this was considered to be the "Pearl of the Carpathian Mountains" and was noted for his good ski runs. *Peles* Castle is also located here but we didn't get an opportunity to tour it. Go to www.aibf-net.go.ro/romania/sinaia.htm for more information and to see some cool photos of Romania. (You can also get a panoramic tour of *Bucharest* at www.bucharest-online.com/)."

And so, to the airport and to home, via a stop in Boston to see our East Coast family. It was a great trip with great traveling companions As our Uniworld guide sheet said, "You've seen fortresses, castles, churches, medieval town centers. You've floated through 6,000 years of history starring Romans, Turks, Celts, Franks, Germans, Thracians, Slavs, Gypsies and more. You've seen amazing architecture from different time periods. Eaten great food, broken bread with cultures completely different from your own, but much closer than you would have imagined."

And Connie has reported it thoroughly, competently, and with love!

Chapter 13

CRUISING THE CARIBBEAN - 2007

In the two decades covering 1990s and 2000s, Pat and I made, by ourselves for a change, three West Indies cruises out of San Juan, Puerto Rico. The last of these was a long voyage that ended up in Acapulco. We arrived there to celebrate my 75th birthday via stops in Panama and the Canal, Caracas, Aruba, all in the Gulf of Mexico; and one or two of the many West Indies Caribbean islands SSE of San Juan. In particular, Aruba was perhaps the most interesting. We docked inland, having traversed a strait which led to the significant oil fields. On the left, where we docked was a tourist town. Across the strait, reached by a walking bridge, was a community of houses and shops that could have been directly imported from Holland – very picturesque. The other two excursions from Puerto Rico covered stops at most of the other 20-odd islands in the chain – all somewhat similar. Later you'll get a better feel for what's to be seen – on this 4th trip with friends as traveling companions.

Although we had visited several islands in the Caribbean on previous occasions, our Travel Agent, Brenda from Lodi, easily coaxed us to try yet another, this time out of Miami, instead of San Juan. She promised, and we confirmed, that most of our old traveling companions would be joining us. The 10 day cruise on the now familiar small ship *Oceania* Line would begin on January 2, 2007, and would visit places in waters where we had never been before.

Actually, it was a protracted trip. We left for Boylston, Mass. (near Boston) on Dec. 21, 2006, to spend Xmas with our youngest son Jeff and his family. Then to Florida to spend the New Years holiday with my several Schweiger and Fox family cousins in the Miami area. On Jan 2, we left on our ten - day Caribbean *Oceania* cruise, which will be described herein. Following the cruise, we rented a car and visited another cousin in Naples, then North to Boynton Beach to stay at friends and see more relatives and attend my 65th(!) High School reunion. We ended up driving to Hilton Head Island to visit with Patti's cousin, Frank Clabaugh. And THAT, we said, might be our last trip (and I think it was).

A North Miami cousin drove us to dockside to embark. Although cruise ships normally keep a tight schedule, 60 passengers from California, including our travel agent's mother, were delayed, so we set sail over two hours late. We re-united with our Houston friends and traveling companions, Connie and Janet, and awaited other cruising friends. Sylvia and George Gonzales of New York had called Connie while she was going through security in Houston. They were headed for Miami with a slim chance to get on the ship due to a late departure. Brenda, our travel agent, had a couple "no-shows", and worked her magic with *Oceania* to delay departure until all of her group had arrived. Our home-town friend, Morris Holmes, also a former traveler with the group, and his daughter, Janet completed 'our gang' for this trip. In fact, it was Morris and his late wife Jean who had introduced us to Brenda's group.

From here on, in this travelogue, I am using Connie's description of the happenings. I have changed the tense from her 'Present' to my 'Past'. She gets all the credit and had first dibs at correcting and commenting on my revised edition.

Our ship, the *M/S Regatta* is relatively small. It accommodates 684 passengers and 400 staff. We had earlier sailed on the *Regatta*'s sister ship, the *M/S Insignia,* on our cruise along the west coast of Central and South America. This ship was nearly identical. Deck 4 housed the medical center, some less expensive state rooms and the reception area. There was a large formal dining room and a good-sized theatre on the Deck 5. A couple of shops, a two-sided martini bar and several conversation areas were also on the Deck 5. Each afternoon, if we not in port, a nice stringed quartet played for interested passengers. High tea was served on Deck 10 near the players. It made for a lovely backdrop for our afternoon trek to the theatre so that we could play Trivia. We had become addicted to playing shipboard Trivia on our South American cruise. But this time it was different:

It was the job of the cruise director to emcee the Trivia competition. This time, our cruise director, David, (from Tomball, Texas via L.A.) was a doofus. His lack of charisma and personality was the opposite of what one would expect a cruise director to be. The cruise director should reflect the hospitality of the cruise line. Such friendliness and charisma can engage a passenger so much that they would want to sail on this same line again and would tell their friends about their good experience. But David Doofus was non-convivial and downright insulting on several occasions. Definitely the wrong man for the job, as many passengers would later say.

But, despite the Doofus, we managed to have fun. However, the much larger group, calling themselves 'The Dorothy's', tended to get more points than any other team. I had optimistically (over Connie and Janet's objection) named our team 'The Winners'. The Winners were losers on most days, but not the biggest losers. The Dorothy's were composed of gay/lesbian passengers, who also had regular 'meetings', just as the AA does.

More about the ship: Deck 9 had the outdoor area with pool, sauna, deck chairs, a bar and a stage, plus a terrific little snack bar called *Waves* (hamburgers, hot dogs, panini, ice cream and salad). There was also a communications center where you could check E-mail and take computer classes. There was a sizable work-out/fitness center and a spa/salon. Near *Waves* is the Terrace Café that served a buffet style breakfast each morning with seating both inside and out. A night, the Terrace Café was converted to a Tapas Bar, with little bits of this and that including sushi, roast beef, etc.

Afternoon tea was served at 4:00 each afternoon in the *Horizons* lounge on Deck 10. There are also two restaurants on the other end of the deck, one is called *Toscana* and the other called the *Polo Grill*. Toscana served Italian fare and the Polo was more of a steak house. If you were accommodated on Deck 6 or below, you could only make reservations at each of these restaurants once during your voyage. But, if you were on Deck 7, you could make two visits to each. Those on Deck 8 could go anytime, I suppose. The Grand Dining Room was fine for our group most of the time, although for tables of ten to twelve people, service tended to be slow and it seemed that dinner dragged on and on, with multiple courses.

We arrived at our first Caribbean island. Christopher Columbus named it *Virgin Gorda* (fat Virgin) because the island's silhouette resembles a fat lady lying on her back. We could see the island of *Tortola* in the distance. *Virgin Gorda* was then, and still probably is, the third-largest (8.5 sq. miles) of the British Virgin Islands (BVI), but the second most populous (2,500). We took a tour on our own rather than use the ship's $62 tour program. We 'did' all they did except that we paid about $10 each. We saw Rockefeller's home which is now an upscale hotel (called *Little Dix Bay Resort*) with its private white sand beach. The generous Rockefeller family gave the area called Devil's Bay National Park to the BVI government in the 1960s. The landscape is surprisingly rugged and cactus can be seen everywhere. We learned that while these islands are favorite tropical destinations, there is very little annual rainfall.

We saw an old abandoned copper mine, but it was too far for us have lunch at the Bitter End Yacht Club on the north sound – clearly seen from a vantage point on a far away hill. This club was a favorite of my sailboat crewman, Bob Shaal, and he sailed out of it on two occasions. It turned out it would have been a bit difficult and a long haul to reach and we didn't have all day in this port-of-call. The last tender was scheduled to depart at 5:30. We contented ourselves with a sprightly, bumpy and windy ride through Spanish Town and on to the legendary *Baths*, near the southwest end of the island.

The *Baths* were quite a sight! Unlike springs or geysers, the *Baths* were actually a beach area that was formed by volcanic activity probably about the same time the island was formed. The volcanoes had strewn huge granite boulders along the beach and there were large caves or grottoes that you could explore, if you don't mind crawling a little and walking carefully. There were also large pools of seawater beneath some of the giant boulders providing swimming opportunities. The *Baths* really were an intriguing site and the water certainly was azure in color, just as our brochures had promised. George, Sylvia and Connie stripped to their bathing suits and enjoyed the waves as they broke over some of the smaller boulders. The *Baths* are the island's main tourist attraction, other than some beautiful but hard-to-access beaches and some pretty bays and more yacht clubs.

There is a small airport on the island. Our guide told us that no pilot, regardless of how skilled, could land there on the first pass. It took a couple of practice runs, because the planes have to come in quite low and the runway is very short. Indeed, a plane came in for a landing so low that it felt like he was just a few feet over our heads! If you had the time, you could ferry between Road Town, Tortola (very close by) and Spanish Town as well as from Trellis Bay on Beef Island to Leverick Bay and Biras Creek; and also catch a ferry to the Bitter End Yacht Club. The *Gorda Peak* National Park is on the north end of Virgin Gorda. Mosquito and Prickly Pear Islands are to the north. Rum is a popular tourist purchase and *Cruzan Dark* was advertised as a great painkiller! Although shopping was limited here, there was a Pusser's Company Store that sold books, nautical items and, of course, the famed *Pusser's Rum*.

After our brief stay on Virgin Gorda, we took the tender back to the ship and agreed to meet-up with our group for dinner in the grand dining room. Following dinner, Connie and I went to the first evening show, featuring the four young on-board entertainers and the ship's 12-piece orchestra. The show was called the *"50s & 60s Stroll Down Memory Lane*" The foursome performed portions of about 60 songs in as many minutes, along with some dancing and a few simple costume changes. We left before John Ferrentino performed his comedy/magic act. While watching the show, a photo of Frank Sinatra was flashed on the background screen and I leaned over to Connie and said, "Did I ever tell you about the time I met Frank Sinatra?" Soon a photo of Grace Kelly was shown and this time I said, "Did I ever tell you about the time I met Grace Kelly?" The story is that the Kelly's were friends of my parents, as well as friends of the parents of my best friend. I went to his sister's wedding at his house, and Grace

Kelly was a guest. She was just beginning her film career and she was quite beautiful...as beautiful as she appeared later on the screen. Frank Sinatra was performing at the same wedding reception. Seems his career had been in the dumpster for a while and a family friend had helped him get out of his going-no-where contract with Tommy Dorsey and sign a new contract with CBS, who owned Capitol Records.

On the 5th day of the cruise we arrived at *St. Barths*. St. Barth is actually St. Barthelemy French West Indies, but islanders have shortened it to St. Barths (still called St. Barth in the U.S.). We took a ship's tender to *Gustavia*, where there were lots of high-end shops. Later saw another concentration of shops as we passed *St. Jean* on the other side of the island. St. Barths is a duty free port, but there was nothing free here. Most everything was very expensive, as might be expected seeing the number of yachts anchored in the beautiful bays. One such was not much smaller than our ship and was outfitted with a helicopter, as well as another little boat in back that was the size of some of the "yachts" in Marina Del Rey. St. Barths' website has an illustration of a stack of money with wings on it. So they are advertising the fact that this is a pricey stop.

And here – sad to say – Connie's account inexplicitly ran out – along with my memory. We recall that we visited one or two more islands in the chain and then headed west – back towards Miami. On the way, we stopped at a port in Honduras and at Grand Turk. The latter is a lovely little island with a great wide beach and a 'boardwalk' which we walked along. The main feature was the at or near the port of embarkment, where there is a shopping center and other stands. The main show was the fabulous Jimmy Buffet surfer style bar and swimming pool – all very luxurious. The establishment was called 'Margaritaville'. We spent most of our time there, watching the lovelies. We have pictures and camcorder records amongst our souvenirs.

Chapter 14

APOLOGIES- 2014

If you look at the Table of Contents, you will notice that there are large time gaps when no trips were reported. Alas, blame the Holocaust. At least five trip stories were lost, and – as I said at the outcome – I just don't have the strength or will to revive/rewrite them. Some of them occurred during this gap. Even as bad, a 20 year span of pictures in my 'Picture Gallery' was wiped out! Thus, most of the pictures in the book come from faded pics that we found in Patti's trip write-ups. By memory, I will sketch the most important of the missing adventures:

All in all, we lived in Haifa for two full semesters plus at least 3 additional months during several non-teaching visits. During these visits, we saw all of Israel and most of Egypt and Jordan worth seeing. The book does cover the Egyptian adventure and gives a bit on Petra and Jerash, and the 'around the world' story provides some insight on Israel. It is the latter country, however, where there are biblical and historical sites that are never to be forgotten. In Jerusalem, in addition to the old inner city, there is *Yad Vashem*, the real holocaust memorial, and the regal King David hotel. Nearby are Bethlehem, Jericho, and Nazareth – all filled with splendiferous sites. Caesarea, the old Roman city and adjacent Coliseum, Jaffa and Tel Aviv - a stark reminder of the old and the new; Zefat (Safed) with its battle scarred buildings and ancient synagogues; the old port of

Acco, where I would sail to on Saturdays; the great beauty of the upper Golan Heights; the Druze villages; the Dead Sea, Masada, and Eilat; and so many more must be seen. They may be alluded to, but not written about.

Also missing are the many trips we made to Europe during the 80s, when I would give a paper to the IAF (International Aerospace Federation) every other year, always visiting with our friends in Esslingen, Heidelberg, Aachen and Paris, including a trip to Russia (or Soviet Union, as it was known then) when we visited Moscow and Baku on the Caspian Sea. At the latter, restaurants served caviar and vodka like others serve bread and butter. We also lost accounts of our trips to Alaska, to Vienna and Spain and Malaysia. By mutual decision, we decided to omit all US internal trips – of which there were many.

We also apologize for the paucity of pictures. We have the pictures, and you can se them if you visit us. However, we limited the number to 20 for financial reasons. You can find appropriate pictures and information on all the sites on Wikipedia.

Finally, one more story needs to be told in full – an old favorite 'travel' story:

One of the favorite authors' of my youth was John O'Hara. His 'Appointment in Samarra' was very good, although not his best. However, its forward, an anecdote about a desperate traveler, forever stays in my mind. It is attributed to W. Somerset Maughn:

DEATH SPEAKS

There was a merchant in Bagdad who sent his servant to market to buy provisions and in a little while the servant came back, white and trembling and said, "Master, just now when I was in the market-place I was jostled by a woman in the crowd and when I turned I saw it was Death that jostled me. She looked at me and made a threatening gesture. Now lend me your horse and I will ride away from this city and avoid my fate. I will go to Samarra and there Death will not find me. The master lent him his horse, and the servant mounted it, and he dug his spurs in its flanks and as fast as the horse could gallop he went. Then the merchant went down to the market-place and he saw me standing in the crowd, and he came to me and said, "Why did you make a threatening gesture to my servant when you saw him this morning?" That was not a threatening gesture, I said, it was only a start of surprise. I was astonished to see him in Bagdad, for I had an appointment with him in Samarra."

THE END

PICTURE INDEX

Made in the USA
Middletown, DE
22 January 2015